The Happiness Formula

CENTENNIAL BOOKS

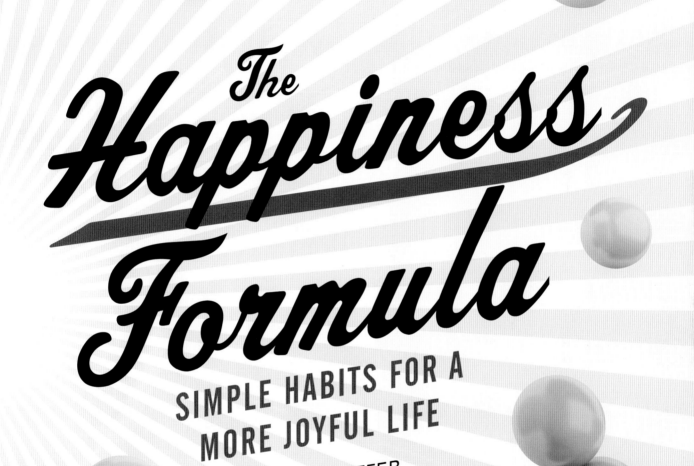

The Happiness Formula

SIMPLE HABITS FOR A
MORE JOYFUL LIFE

ALYSSA SHAFFER

CONTENTS

PART 1
WHY HAPPINESS MATTERS

8 — The Science of Happiness

16 — The Health Benefits of Being Happy

24 — Global Joy

32 — The Upside of Feeling Bad

40 — Live Your Best Life

PART 2
THE PURSUIT OF HAPPINESS

50 — The Kindness Connection

58 — The Importance of Resilience

66 — Staying Positive

74 — The Happiness Conundrum

82 — How to Raise Joyful Kids

90 — Find Your Happy Place

PART 3
CULTIVATING YOUR BLISS

100 — Beat the Monday Blahs

104 — Love the Work You Do

114 — Clean Slate

122 — A Call to Action

PART 4
EASY WAYS TO FIND YOUR JOY

130 — Happiness Hacks

142 — Feel-Good Moves

150 — Hugging It Out

158 — Head First

166 — 8 On-the-Go Meditations

170 — Why Laughter Is the Best Medicine

178 — Pet Project

PART 1
WHY HAPPINESS MATTERS
PROOF THAT YOUR MINDSET REALLY CAN CHANGE YOUR LIFE

THE
SCIENCE OF
HAPPINESS

RESEARCHERS SAY THE DEFINITION
CAN SHIFT FROM PERSON
TO PERSON, BUT AT ITS CORE,
TRUE JOY IS DEPENDENT ON
YOUR CONNECTION TO OTHERS

WHY HAPPINESS MATTERS

→ **HAPPINESS:** It's the thing most of us feel we should have more of. And that's not just because being happy is associated with feeling good. According to decades of research, happy people tend to live longer, exhibit fewer or less severe mental health issues, have more friends and perform better at work. But what, exactly, is happiness, when we get down to defining it? And is striving to obtain more of it really the best way to increase our well-being?

For starters, happiness for one person may not be the same as for another—especially if those individuals hail from separate cultures. Consider the differences between Eastern and Western emotion concepts: Westerners typically predicate happiness on individual experiences of pleasurable feelings and personal freedom to pursue and realize their own unique potential. Meanwhile, those with a more Eastern orientation (think: Buddhists, Hindus and Taoists, to name just a few) typically view happiness as the result of dissolved boundaries between the self and a larger whole or higher power.

Eastern perspectives seem to be backed by science. "There's more and more evidence accumulating that focusing on others makes us much happier than focusing on ourselves," says Kristin Layous, Ph.D., an assistant professor of psychology at California State University. In her studies, Layous compared the effects of trying to make someone else happier to the effects of trying to make ourselves happier. She found subjects who exerted more effort trying to brighten others' days felt happier than those who tried to brighten their own.

That isn't to say doing things to bolster your own well-being detracts from happiness—nor is trying to please everyone in your life the key to 24-7 bliss. (It's not. According to research, it can heighten interpersonal stress and lead to depression, especially in women.) But if helping someone else feel a little bit better can help *us* feel a whole lot better, that says a lot about enhanced subjective well-being.

Layous points out that going beyond ourselves to help others solidifies our own sense of feeling important and useful while also strengthening social bonds. We feel intrinsically motivated and alive—a psychological state many of us would categorize as "happy."

But Western ideas of happiness aren't completely off the mark. Our values of autonomy (the degree to which we feel we're making our own choices) and competence (how effective we feel we are) are two of three fundamental needs proposed by psychologists Edward L. Deci and Richard M. Ryan in their theory of self-determination. (Relatedness—being connected to others—is the third.)

But that sense of being happy doesn't equate with the absence of pain and other negative emotions, notes Brock Bastian, Ph.D., author of *The Other Side of Happiness*. "You need a contrasting experience, like pain, in order to appreciate pleasure," he notes.

Although we may not be consciously aware of it, most of us regularly seek out pain and other nonpleasurable emotions. Think: pushing through a tough workout to feel the euphoria of a runner's high, or taking on the stress of a full-time job in order to have meaningful work.

Pain (in the form of physical suffering, emotional adversity or sometimes both) can also help bring individuals closer together and boost the odds of cooperation, even among

The field of positive psychology seeks to explore the very nature of what makes us happy.

strangers. Bastian and colleagues from the University of Queensland had groups of undergrads submerge their hands in either buckets of ice water (the "pain" condition) or in room-temperature water (the "nonpain" condition). Those who had undergone the more excruciating submersion were more likely to report feeling part of, and loyal to, their group than did the nonpain group. In a separate study, those who reported feeling higher levels of pain were more likely to choose a payout option in an economic game that benefited all group members rather than the individual.

"Negative experiences are a fundamental part of affiliating with others," Bastian explains. "Expressing our pain is a way to get empathy from others—it triggers social bonding."

Another mistake most of us make in our ongoing quest for happiness? Pressuring

"THERE'S MORE AND MORE EVIDENCE ACCUMULATING THAT FOCUSING ON OTHERS MAKES US MUCH HAPPIER THAN FOCUSING ON OURSELVES."

—PSYCHOLOGIST KRISTIN LAYOUS, PH.D.

Strengthening relationships with those around you can help boost your sense of purpose and meaning.

ourselves to feel happier than we already are and (apologies to our Founding Fathers) setting happiness as a goal in and of itself.

In a 2015 study, Bastian found that people who believed others disapproved of their negative emotions were more likely to feel lonely. And in two studies published in the journal *Depression and Anxiety*, Bastian also discovered that the perceived pressure to be happy can exacerbate symptoms of depression and increase rumination over failure.

"Constantly taking your own pulse and asking 'Am I happy yet?' is more likely to undermine your happiness than breed a lasting version of it," Layous adds. And pursuing material items purely for the purpose of achieving happiness can also lead us astray. Remember that car, dress or home you were convinced would bring you happiness? Chances are its positive effects were short-lived.

So what can we do to feel happier? In addition to engaging in activities that benefit others, pursuing meaningful experiences through work or hobbies can increase how often people report feeling happy. Take time to appreciate what you have, seek out positive stimuli—nature, if that's your thing; a good laugh, if that gets you going; pets, if they make you smile; baking, reading or any other activity that floats your boat—and you may be able to change your happiness levels for good, insists Layous.

The most important change we can all make may just be to accept that happiness isn't a constant, that we are free to define it for ourselves and needn't kick ourselves when we don't feel as happy as we think we should be—or as happy as we assume (perhaps falsely) other people are.

5 PROVEN WAYS TO BOOST YOUR MOOD

HAPPINESS CERTAINLY CAN SEEM ELUSIVE. BUT MASTERING A FEW NEW HABITS CAN DO WONDERS FOR HOW GREAT YOU FEEL ON A REGULAR BASIS. HERE ARE SCIENCE-BACKED STRATEGIES TO MAKE YOU SMILE EVERY DAY

1 COUNT YOUR BLESSINGS

Writing down three good things that happen to you each day— detailing who was involved, what was said and how you believe the positive event came about—has been found to effectively boost people's moods. Try it daily for a few weeks and track what a difference it makes.

2 GET MOVING

Physical activity not only helps you feel better in the short term, studies show it can stave off unhappiness over the long haul. Add a brisk walk to your daily routine, a short yoga practice to your morning or a few exercise classes to your week to reap physical and mental health benefits.

3 PRIORITIZE PEOPLE

Social interactions have a significant impact on how happy we feel by improving our sense of connectedness and value. Close friends and family members (whom we get along with) boost our sense of meaning, purpose and well-being. But so, too, do the "weaker" ties we have to folks we regularly interact with. If you're in need of a quick pick-me-up, chat up your barista or reach out to an acquaintance you haven't heard from in a while.

4 LEARN TO KNIT

Or find another hobby that makes you smile—having a leisurely pursuit has been shown to increase overall happiness. Some experts think this is due to the intense focus achieved when we take part in activities that give us just the right amount of challenge. For starters, try gardening, hiking, painting, taking an improv class or learning a new instrument.

5 MEDITATE ON IT

Various types of meditation have been found to increase mindfulness, a state linked to fewer experiences of stress, fewer symptoms of anxiety and depression, and better tolerance of pain. The mindfulness brought about by meditation has also been found to increase feelings of life satisfaction, positive emotions and self-compassion. Try watching a guided meditation video on YouTube or find a mindfulness meditation class nearby.

THE HEALTH BENEFITS OF BEING HAPPY

WHY THOSE POSITIVE FEELINGS CAN GIVE YOUR BODY A BOOST

→ **HAPPINESS FEELS** pretty darn good. But what's really going on in your body when you experience positive emotions, and can those changes help keep you healthy day after day? Research shows that positivity can have a substantial influence on your overall well-being and may even help you live longer. Following are a few of the many benefits of feeling happy.

YOUR BRAIN GETS TRAINED TO BE MORE POSITIVE

Always feel like you have a grin on your face? It's not a surprise: Researchers say that the happier you feel, the more you tend to stay that way. "Being positive helps you form new pathways in the brain, so it becomes easier and easier to reach that state again," says Gabriella Farkas, M.D., Ph.D., a psychiatrist and behavioral health specialist in New York City.

Positive psychology researcher Barbara Fredrickson, Ph.D., has coined the "broaden and build theory" which postulates that micro-moments of positivity (small things that make you happy day in and day out) can accumulate over time. So while that smile after saying "hi" to a neighbor may not last, having positive interactions every day will make it even easier to keep smiling. In other words, positivity accumulates over time, so feeling good today helps you feel as good—if not better—tomorrow. Happiness is also associated with a boost in brain function, says Dr. Farkas, including several systems that become more active when you experience positive emotions.

YOU'LL SEE THE DOCTOR LESS

A summary of more than 150 studies published in *Health Psychology Review* looked at the impact of well-being on objective health outcomes and found that feelings of well-being were linked to positive short- and long-term outcomes.

Other research has shown that being in a good mood can boost your immune system. A British study discovered that the flu vaccine was more effective at preventing the flu among subjects who reported being in a positive mood when they received the vaccination. And a study from Carnegie Mellon University found subjects who were happy were less likely to catch colds compared to those who reported feeling depressed, nervous or angry. Even those happy individuals who did get sick had fewer or less severe symptoms compared to their more somber peers.

THE BODY POSITIVE

HERE'S A LOOK AT WHAT'S HAPPENING IN YOUR BODY WHEN YOU START TO FEEL HAPPY, ACCORDING TO PSYCHIATRIST GABRIELLA FARKAS, M.D., PH.D.

- PUPILS GET WIDER
- FACIAL MUSCLES RELAX
- HEART RATE DECREASES
- BREATHING SLOWS AND DEEPENS
- FEEL-GOOD CHEMICALS SUCH AS ENDORPHINS AND SEROTONIN ARE RELEASED
- DIGESTION IMPROVES

A good mood can make your quality of life better year after year.

YOUR HEART WILL WORK BETTER

Happiness feels like it comes from the heart, so it's no surprise that it also makes your ticker function better. A study in the journal *Neurobiology of Aging* found happiness was inversely related to high blood pressure and that men who reported feeling greater levels of happiness had lower heart rates (about six beats slower per minute among the happiest participants). A British study found that patients who rated themselves as happiest had a healthier pattern of heart rate variability (the amount of time between heart beats, often used as an indicator of heart disease risk) when their hearts were evaluated. A Canadian study discovered that participants who rated themselves with lower levels of anger and stress were less likely to develop heart disease than those who reported less positive feelings. And a 2007 Harvard School of Public Health study that followed more than 6,000 men and women for 20 years found that emotional vitality (a sense of energy, positive well-being and an ability to deal with stress) reduced the risk of coronary heart disease even after controlling for positive behaviors like exercise and not smoking.

YOUR HORMONES BECOME MORE UPBEAT

We all know about the "fight or flight" response that kicks in when you're under stress, whether you're running late because you're stuck in a traffic jam or you're being yelled at by your boss. "Happiness helps to flip the script," says Partha Nandi, M.D., the author of *Ask Dr. Nandi* and creator of a syndicated talk show on patient advocacy. People who are more positive tend to have a lower stress response, he says, and higher levels of feel-good hormones like endorphins that help you feel relaxed. Research also shows that happy people have about 23 percent lower levels of the stress hormone cortisol compared to the least happy people. And a 2009 study found that of subjects who went through a stressful situation, those who reported feeling the happiest overall recovered the quickest compared to their least upbeat peers.

WHY IT'S OKAY TO BE BUMMED OUT

Having the occasional off day is okay when it comes to your health. Research from UC Berkeley, published in the *Journal of Personality and Social Psychology,* found people who habitually accept having negative emotions actually experience fewer of these down days, which will eventually add up to better health. Researchers speculate that people who commonly put off their darker times end up feeling more psychologically—and therefore physically—stressed. So go ahead, feel blue every once in a while: Just don't wait too long until you start smiling again.

Clinical depression can take a serious toll on your health, so it's important to get help if the blues don't go away.

WHY HAPPINESS MATTERS

YOU'LL BE MORE COMFORTABLE

People who report having the highest levels of positive emotions are less likely to experience increases in pain from chronic conditions like arthritis, according to a 2005 study from Arizona State University. And a 2001 study from the *Journal of Research in Personality* found those who reported the highest level of positive emotions such as a good mood were the least likely to experience negative symptoms like muscle strain, dizziness and heartburn.

YOU'LL SLEEP BETTER

You're obviously grumpier after a bad night's sleep, but the reverse is also true: When you're grumpy (or anxious or stressed), you'll sleep less well. And the happier your state of mind, the easier it is to fall asleep. "Feeling joyful can help you sleep better, while helping alleviate a bad mood and the stress that comes with it," says Dr. Nandi.

YOU'LL LIVE LONGER— AND FEEL BETTER DOING IT

Why keep a smile on your face? You'll get more out of your golden years. A 2011 British study found adults age 52 to 79 who reported the highest levels of feeling happy, excited or content were 35 percent less likely to die over the course of the five-year study period than the least happy subjects. And a 2008 Australian study of nearly 10,000 adults found that those who reported being happier or more satisfied with their lives were about 1.5 times less likely to develop chronic health conditions.

RESEARCH HAS SHOWN THAT BEING IN A GOOD MOOD CAN BOOST YOUR IMMUNE SYSTEM.

Happiness is contagious— and it just may be the secret to living a longer, healthier life.

GLOBAL JOY

WHAT CAN WE LEARN FROM THE HAPPIEST COUNTRIES? *(SPOILER ALERT: THE U.S. ISN'T ONE OF THEM)*

→ **DISNEYLAND ASIDE,** Finland is the happiest place on earth—followed closely by Denmark, Norway, Iceland and the Netherlands. That's according to the 2019 "World Happiness Report," an annual study of reported life satisfaction around the world. The report, which has been released annually for the past five years, evaluates about 3,000 responses from 155 countries.

Researchers found six economic and social factors (freedom, generosity, health, social support, income and trustworthy governance) explained most of the variation in happiness levels around the globe. The U.S. continues to slip down in the rankings, coming in 19th. Although income and healthy life expectancy levels increased in the U.S. since the last survey, all four social categories (perceived freedom, generosity, social support and trust in government) went down. "The central paradox...is this: Income per person in the U.S. has increased roughly three times since 1960, but measured happiness has not risen," researchers wrote.

Money, at least in the U.S., is definitely not able to buy happiness, according to the report. "The situation [in the U.S.] has gotten worse in recent years: Per capita GDP [gross domestic product] is still rising, but happiness is now actually falling." And the report points to politicians whose efforts focus mostly on improving the economy, saying that's not the only issue that needs attention. "The United States can and should raise happiness by addressing America's multifaceted social crisis—rising inequality, corruption, isolation and distrust— rather than focusing exclusively or even mainly on economic growth," writes Jeffrey D. Sachs, director of the Center for Sustainable Develop-

HOW DO RESEARCHERS MEASURE WORLD HAPPINESS?

WEALTH
GDP per capita, or a measure of a country's economic output. Researchers take the gross domestic product and divide it by a country's total population as a way to measure the overall standard of living.

HEALTH
Evaluates healthy life expectancy at birth based on data from the World Health Organization.

SOCIAL SUPPORT
Determines the national average in a poll that asks "If you were in trouble, do you have relatives or friends you can count on to help you whenever you need them, or not?"

FREEDOM TO CHOOSE
Based on the average response to the question, "Are you satisfied or dissatisfied with your freedom to choose what you do with your life?"

GENEROSITY
Based on the average response to the question, "Have you donated money to a charity in the past month?"

CORRUPTION
Based on the average of answers to two questions: "Is corruption widespread through the government or not?" and "Is corruption widespread within business or not?"

DAILY HAPPINESS
An average of previous-day measurements for happiness, laughter and enjoyment, along with the average of previous-day measures for worry, sadness and anger.

Daily enjoyment figures strongly in the happiness equation for every country surveyed.

ment at the Earth Institute, Columbia University.

In other words, there was less social support and less sense of personal freedom, along with less generous donations to people in need and more perceived corruption of government and business. "America's crisis is, in short, a social crisis, not an economic crisis," Sachs writes.

The highest-ranking countries, on the other hand, may have lower economic indicators such as GDP per capita, but they outpace the U.S. on personal freedom, social support and lower perceived corruption. Unfortunately, adds Sachs, economic disparity may be widening our happiness gap. "Income inequality has reached astronomical levels, with the top one percent of American households taking home almost all of the gains in economic growth in recent decades, while the share of the bottom 50 percent plummets."

Other key indicators of happiness, especially in Western countries, include a work-life balance and mental health, as well as having a partner and getting an education. The biggest causes of misery, researchers note, are poverty, low education, unemployment, living alone and physical or mental illness.

The best way to use the report? Think of it as a way to draw global attention to helping countries create sound policy about the biggest issue for most people—our overall well-being, Sachs writes. "This report gives evidence that happiness is a result of creating strong social foundations. It's time to build social trust and healthy lives."

SURPRISING FACTS ABOUT BLISSFUL PLACES

COULD THESE BE SOME OF THE REASONS WHY THE NATIONS BELOW HAVE SUCH HIGH REPORTED MEASURES OF LIFE SATISFACTION?

■ **Norway** was the first country to introduce compulsory paternity leave, giving fathers up to 14 weeks of parental leave as a way to encourage more men to assume greater responsibility in the home.

■ Nearly half of all residents of the **Danish** capital of Copenhagen commute to work daily by bike. There are actually more bicycles in Copenhagen than people—and five times as many bicycles as cars.

■ **Switzerland** is home to more than 400 varieties of cheese, and the average Swiss citizen consumes about 35 pounds of cheese a year (not to mention about 23 pounds of chocolate!).

■ **Iceland** has no standing army, and its police do not carry guns. It also has one of the lowest crime rates of any country, with an annual murder rate of 1.8 a year.

■ According to a 2012 study compiled by the Organization for Economic Cooperation and Development, more than half of **Canadians** have earned a college diploma.

■ Bungee jumping was invented in **New Zealand** in 1988 when two young Kiwis started to experiment with a mix of latex rubber, climbing equipment and parachute harnesses. Today you can leap from bridges, climbs, railways, stadium roofs and platforms perched on cliffs. The highest jump is the Nevis Bungy, which involves a 440-feet (134-meter) plunge.

WHERE DO YOU RANK?

The "World Happiness Report" bases its results on answers from around the globe to a survey run by the polling group Gallup. The poll uses a measurement called the Cantril Self-Anchoring Striving Scale. Here's how it works:

• Imagine a ladder with steps numbered from zero at the bottom to 10 at the top. The top rung represents the best possible life for you. The bottom rung represents the worst possible life for you.

• On which step of the ladder do you personally feel you stand at this time?

• On which step do you think you will stand about five years from now?

■ Recycling is so successful in **Sweden** that only about 4 percent of its waste goes into landfills. Because the country runs a successful waste-to-energy program, neighboring Norway pays Sweden to take its trash, which Sweden then uses to generate about 20 percent of its heat and electricity.

■ There are an estimated 3 million saunas in **Finland**, which only has a population of 5.3 million, and about 99 percent of people visit a sauna at least once a week. Almost everyone uses the sauna naked (you must shower before entering).

■ If you're up for a hefty hike, there's no place better than **Austria**. It's the home of 13 peaks that are more than 10,000 feet high, and there are about 35,000 miles of hiking trails. And about one-third of the forested land is protected from development.

■ Visit a coffee shop in the **Netherlands** and you can buy a joint with your java. Coffee shops are allowed to sell up to 5 grams of cannabis per person per day (but you need to be at least 18 years old to enter).

THE TOP 10
HAPPIEST COUNTRIES

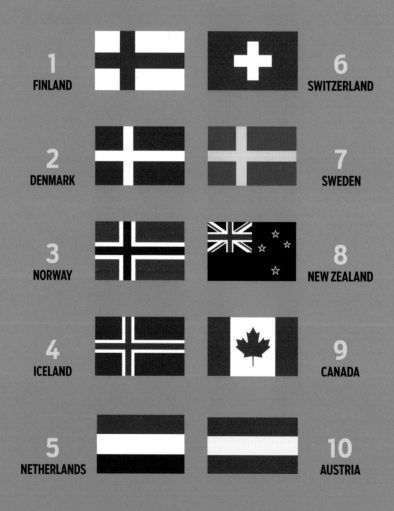

1 FINLAND

2 DENMARK

3 NORWAY

4 ICELAND

5 NETHERLANDS

6 SWITZERLAND

7 SWEDEN

8 NEW ZEALAND

9 CANADA

10 AUSTRIA

AND THE 10 LEAST HAPPY COUNTRIES

1 SOUTH SUDAN

2 CENTRAL AFRICAN REPUBLIC

3 AFGHANISTAN

4 TANZANIA

5 RWANDA

6 YEMEN

7 MALAWI

8 SYRIA

9 BOTSWANA

10 HAITI

Source *"World Happiness Report" 2019*

THE UPSIDE OF FEELING BAD

POSITIVE EMOTIONS MAY FEEL GOOD, BUT EXPERTS SAY THE NEGATIVE ONES ARE IMPORTANT, TOO. HERE'S HOW TO THRIVE WHEN THINGS AREN'T GOING YOUR WAY

WHY HAPPINESS MATTERS

→ **SCROLL THROUGH YOUR INSTAGRAM** or Facebook feed, and chances are most images feature smiling faces. From beaming couples celebrating an engagement to festive groups of friends toasting over drinks, happiness is the name of the social media game. While some do post about more somber topics, overall, positivity outshines negativity.

The problem is, real life isn't always peachy keen. It's full of disappointments, both small and large. Real life throws plenty of curveballs at us, from layoffs to losing loved ones. But in an age when people put only their most perfect moments on display, it's easy to feel as if you're the only one who ever goes through a tough time. Yet you're not alone. And the hard stuff is actually just as important for a life full of happiness as positive experiences. "It would be irrational to think we can rid our lives of all negative experiences," says Michelle Gielan, a positive psychology researcher and author of *Broadcasting Happiness*. "But it's less about what happens and more about what you do about it." Read on to learn about the positive side of negativity and how you can learn to handle it better.

THE PURPOSE OF NEGATIVITY

Despite what countless articles, books and social media suggest, "Human beings are not designed to feel happy all the time," says Sonja Lyubomirsky, Ph.D., a psychology professor at the University of California, Riverside, and author of *The How of Happiness*. Negative emotions serve a purpose, both evolutionarily and emotionally.

Think of emotions such as sadness, stress and anxiety as red flags that your mind wants you to pay attention to. "Sadness and other

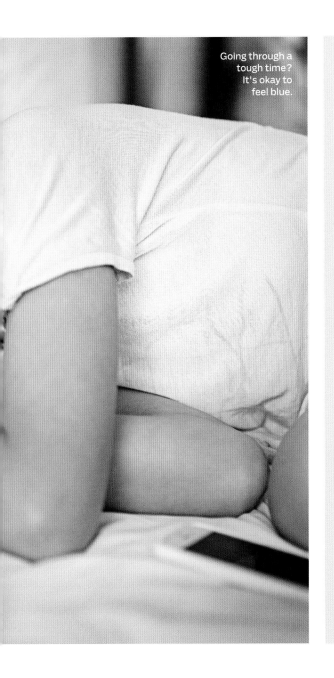

Going through a tough time? It's okay to feel blue.

WHEN IT'S MORE THAN JUST SADNESS

Sadness—a perfectly normal emotion—can usually be tied to a certain situation that's causing you distress. But sometimes a bad mood can progress beyond just the blues. Depression is a medical condition that requires professional help. Talk to a health-care professional if you're experiencing some of the following symptoms for most of the day, nearly every day, for two weeks or more:

▶ Sad thoughts or mood that affect your ability to function in one or more areas of life (such as work or home)

▶ Feelings of guilt, worthlessness or helplessness

▶ Decreased energy or fatigue

▶ Loss of interest in hobbies that previously brought joy

▶ Difficulty sleeping or oversleeping

▶ Difficulty concentrating, remembering or making decisions

▶ Thoughts of death or suicide

Not everyone who is depressed experiences every symptom, according to the National Institute of Mental Health—some people may have only a few while others have many, and no two people are affected in the same way.

One of the leading causes of suicide is depression—as depression deepens, the pain can become overwhelming. Depressive illness can distort thinking so a person can't contemplate clearly. A chemical imbalance in the brain, combined with this sense of despair and hopelessness, can make some people feel like they simply need to end the pain through suicide. If you suspect someone may be suicidal or are having suicidal thoughts yourself, reach out to a crisis hotline and don't be afraid to talk directly about suicide, advises the Suicide Prevention Lifeline. Depression is often treated with medication, talk therapy or a combination of the two. The good news: Even the most severe cases can be treated, and the earlier you begin, the easier it will be to start to feel better.

negative feelings indicate that we need to make a change," Gielan explains. If you're angry, for example, it likely means there's an injustice that you want to correct. If you're anxious, there may be a threat you need to attend to. And if you're sad, it means you care about a situation so deeply that it's causing you distress. Negative feelings can also serve as the catalyst you need to transition to a better place in your life—such as a new job or relationship.

And don't beat yourself up for feeling down. Trying to repress negative moods can actually make you feel worse, according to research. People who accept their emotions—both dark and light—without judgment are better able to cope with stress and feel better in the long run.

Remember, happiness isn't static—it's more about moving toward goals than achieving them. "Happiness is the joy we feel as we grow toward our potential," Gielan adds.

LIVING IN THE GRAY

It's easy to try to sort things that happen into neat categories—either good or bad. "We have a tendency to be obsessed with extremes: We're either happy or sad, dieting or not dieting, rich or poor," says Cheri Augustine Flake, L.C.S.W., a therapist in Atlanta.

But life isn't always so black-and-white. Focusing on either end of the spectrum ignores the in-between part, or the gray area, as Flake calls it. The gray area is actually an exciting, even fun, place to be, and it signals you're changing and transitioning, even if things haven't fallen perfectly into place. After all, the happiest people in the world wouldn't feel that way if they didn't also know what it was like to feel blue. "We grow

and we become who we're supposed to be," Flake says. "No one says it's easy. But they *do* say, 'I went through this tough thing and I got better because of it.'"

In other words, we get so wrapped up in how things should go down that we don't see the opportunity in less-than-ideal situations. "The strange thing about the worst things that happen to us is that they can sometimes become the best things that could happen to us," Flake notes.

HOW TO GET THROUGH THE WORST OF TIMES

This isn't to say that negative situations, like a breakup, aren't difficult. But the experts reveal there are some strategies to help you navigate the rough waters of life. For starters, try to simply focus on the present moment. "Even if

3:1

OPTIMAL RATIO OF POSITIVE TO NEGATIVE EMOTION IN YOUR DAY-TO-DAY LIFE, ACCORDING TO POSITIVITY PSYCHOLOGY RESEARCHER BARBARA FREDRICKSON OF THE UNIVERSITY OF NORTH CAROLINA. (TEST YOURS AT POSITIVITYRATIO.COM)

A change of scenery,
especially going outside,
can sometimes help get
you out of a funk.

WHY HAPPINESS MATTERS

Lift your spirits with creative hobbies that take your mind off your troubles.

you're weeping and crying, can you just be okay with that?" Flake asks.

And remind yourself that you are safe and sound: "If you're sitting in your car, for example, feel the back of your legs touching the seat. Feel the cool air-conditioning blowing on you," she suggests. "This helps remind your brain that everything is okay—that you can find some peace, no matter what else is going on."

You can also seek some good old-fashioned distractions from your problems. This doesn't mean putting your head in the sand or turning to vices like drugs or alcohol, but rather allow yourself to feel fully absorbed in something else, Lyubomirsky says. During a rough patch, take time out of your day to do something enjoyable—perhaps see a movie, work on a creative hobby or go to your favorite restaurant. "This can allow you to take a breather, refresh yourself, and then come back and address the problems," she notes.

Finally, take small steps to deal with the issue at hand. "When we're facing a problem, many of us, women especially, tend to ruminate and get stuck imagining the worst," Gielan explains. But the best thing we can do is to focus on what she calls a "now step"—a small, meaningful action you can take right now, even if it may not solve the problem completely. If, for example, you need a new car but you can't afford it, consider what you *can* do at this moment. It can be as simple as opting for the small coffee instead of a mocha grande. That won't solve all your money problems, but "a small step like that allows your brain to register a small 'win,' moving you forward from the problem to what you can do about it right now," Gielan says. And moving forward is really what happiness is all about.

WHY HAPPINESS MATTERS

LIVE YOUR BEST LIFE

MAXIMIZE YOUR CONTENTMENT AT EVERY AGE

→ **SOME OF YOUR** best years are yet to come—at least according to most research on how our level of happiness changes throughout our lives.

Numerous studies have found that happiness follows a U-shaped curve as we age. Although joy appears to decline from about early adulthood to midlife, our mood swings upward again and continues to increase as we settle into our later stages of life. That's right: Your peak years of happiness seem to be not only when you are young, in great health and having fun but also again in retirement when your mind and body may not be as sharp and fit, but you have a new outlook and want to make every moment count.

That's no reason to think the years in between need to be a bummer, though. "Happiness is subjective. What makes one person happy or content may be different from what makes someone else happy," says Dilip V. Jeste, M.D., senior associate dean for healthy aging and distinguished professor of psychiatry and neurosciences at the University of California, San Diego. "And people's expectations about happiness change." As you journey from one phase of life to the next, follow this advice to make every age a golden one.

WHY HAPPINESS MATTERS

Whether you work solo or in a group, make a commitment to achieve your best.

YOUR

20s

THERE IS TREMENDOUS PRESSURE, AND WE FEEL AS IF WE'RE NOT DOING AS WELL AS OUR PEERS IN OUR 20S. WE STRIVE TO IMPRESS OTHERS AND BE ACCEPTED BY OTHERS.... YOU WANT TO APPEAR TO BE IN CHARGE, YET YOU'RE ANXIOUS ABOUT ALL OF THIS.

Graduating from college and starting your first job is a time of both great excitement and also stress. "The 20s are the 'fountain of youth' from a physical point of view, but not from a mental-health one," Dr. Jeste says. "There is a lot of stress, depression and anxiety during that time." Still, you can turn some of this excitement into happiness. "When you're in your 20s, you are future-focused," explains Cassie Mogilner Holmes, Ph.D., professor of marketing at UCLA Anderson School of Management. "You have the motivation to start new things, expose yourself to new experiences and try out a lot of exciting and challenging things."

So do that in both your career and your dating. Take chances—because you can—and try not to fall prey to peer pressure and keeping up with your peers on social media.

Dr. Jeste suggests focusing on what you can control—doing your best, getting into the best school you can, starting a good job—and ignoring what you can't, such as how many people like your Facebook page or how much you earn compared to others.

IT'S IMPORTANT TO BE SURE
YOU'RE BEING VALUABLE
TO SOMEONE ELSE. FORM AND
CULTIVATE RELATIONSHIPS,
NOT JUST AT WORK BUT IN ALL
ASPECTS OF LIFE, WHERE
YOU HAVE SOMETHING TO OFFER
THAT SOMEONE ELSE WANTS.

YOUR
30s

The third decade of life is when many people establish themselves in their careers. Whether that's continuing down the path you studied in college, becoming an entrepreneur or being a wife or husband, the secret to job happiness lies in the four Cs, says George Vaillant, M.D., coauthor of *Heaven on My Mind: Using the Harvard Grant Study of Adult Development to Explore the Value of the Prospection of Life After Death.*

   "You want to find something you are competent at, committed to, compensated for and contented with," says the Harvard Medical School psychiatry professor. "A job isn't just something you get paid for. Look in the mirror and realize why you do what you do." It's also important to be sure you're being valuable to someone else. Form and cultivate your relationships—not just at work but in all aspects of life—where you have something to offer that someone else wants.

   Set high but attainable expectations of yourself. "Happiness comes from trying to do better," Dr. Jeste says, "but your expectations also have to be realistic.

Find a job that keeps you engaged and makes you feel valued.

Happiness in your 40s is often about finding peace and calm.

YOUR
40s

Once you hit the big 40, society seems to make it loud and clear that it's all downhill from here. Walk down a greeting card aisle and you'll see that 40th-birthday cards often use biting humor, Dr. Jeste notes. In addition to trying to fulfill society's expectations, oftentimes 40-somethings are performing a balancing act of caring for both their children and their aging parents.

It can help to embrace that what made you happy in your 20s likely isn't going to give you satisfaction now—which is normal. Having a family and a career is exhausting, so while staying in on Friday to watch an animated movie seemed boring when you were in your first postcollege relationship, now it may be just the thing to make you happy.

"Don't feel guilty about it," Mogilner Holmes says. Her research has found that for younger people, happiness tends to be associated with excitement. But as you hit your 30s, things start to shift, and in your 40s and beyond, happiness is more about feeling calm, peaceful and content.

Some of that comes from savoring the accomplishments you've achieved in your life. "Start to enjoy your success and be content with it and find happiness in that," she adds.

YOUR
50s

Our culture makes it seem like you wake up on your 50th birthday and suddenly want to move to a small village in Costa Rica to open up a dog shelter. And yes, some people experience a midlife crisis. "You have settled into your life and start feeling like you didn't accomplish what you set out to do," Dr. Jeste says.

If you find yourself wanting a drastic change or feeling depressed, first note who you are comparing yourself with. "Don't compare your health with your health in your 20s—compare it to that of your peers," Dr. Jeste says. You'll probably realize that most of them are in the same situation as you.

So remember there's a lot to celebrate. "Nobody gets everything in life, but you've managed quite a bit," Dr. Jeste says. "You can make a lot of use of the rest of your life." Sure, you may not be able to, say, run a marathon. But how about a half-marathon or a relay with friends or your kids?

SEEK OUT NEW HOBBIES, TRAVEL, LEARN A NEW INSTRUMENT OR LANGUAGE OR DO OTHER THINGS THAT YOU NOW HAVE MONEY AND TIME FOR.

YOUR

60s

Seniors are often the most content of any age.

The closer we get to retirement, the more we shift from being me-focused to being other-focused. "As people get older, we start to feel greater happiness from a sense of purpose and meaning, and part of that is having an impact outside of ourselves," Mogilner Holmes says. This can lead to philanthropic pursuits and general greater generosity.

Find something that allows you to give back in a way that you enjoy. Perhaps you'd like to work to raise money for an international organization, volunteer with a local boys and girls club or help to raise your grandchildren. "This not only gives you a sense of purpose, it helps you leave a legacy, too," Dr. Jeste says.

AS WE GET OLDER, WE START TO FEEL GREATER HAPPINESS FROM A SENSE OF PURPOSE... HAVING AN IMPACT OUTSIDE OF OURSELVES.

YOUR
70s

LONELINESS MAKES OLDER PEOPLE UNHAPPY. AFTER RETIREMENT, YOU TEND TO LOSE CONTACT WITH PEERS AND YOU MAY LOSE YOUR PARTNER. IT'S CRITICAL TO HAVE SOME OTHER SOCIAL CONTACT.

You may not be in the best shape of your life physically in your 70s, but that doesn't mean you can't be in the best shape of your life in other ways. "We found people at 70 are less depressed than people are at 40," Dr. Vaillant says. Dr. Jeste's research on adults aged 21 to 100 led to similar findings. "Older people had more physical disabilities and memory problems, but they also had greater happiness, satisfaction with life and quality of well-being," he says.

To experience these perks, it's essential to maintain relationsips. "Loneliness makes older people unhappy, and after retirement you lose contact with peers and you may lose your partner," Dr. Jeste says. "It's critical to have some other social contact."

In addition to pursuing any work that contributes to society, you may find that what seemed mundane in your 20s is now the calm contentment you crave. Perhaps that's gardening with a neighbor or enjoying a weekly potluck with your church. "Older people realize that time is precious and our lives are limited, and they become more deliberate in how they spend time and extract happiness from it," Mogilner Holmes says. Find what makes you happy and relish it.

PART 2

THE PURSUIT OF HAPPINESS
WHY IT'S NOT AS HARD AS YOU MAY THINK

PURSUIT OF HAPPINESS

THE KINDNESS CONNECTION

DOING UNTO OTHERS IN A POSITIVE WAY CAN ALSO HELP IMPROVE YOUR OWN LEVELS OF HEALTH AND HAPPINESS

→ **EVER NOTICE THAT** little burst of positivity you get when you hold the door for a stranger, smile at the checkout cashier or wave the car across from you to make a turn first? Some simply call small acts like these politeness or good manners, but they're also expressions of kindness. And they can go a long way toward making you a happier and more satisfied human.

"We are wired for kindness and compassion," notes Tara Cousineau, Ph.D., a psychologist based in Milton, Massachusetts, and the author of *The Kindness Cure.* "These qualities are fundamental to our survival as a species. We would not have thrived over eons without collaborative emotions."

But in our ever-busy world, with pressures at home, work and pretty much everywhere else we turn, our instinct to be compassionate can sometimes be stymied. "When you are under stress, the natural response is to go into a protective mode," says Cousineau. We tend to snap at others and get more caught up in our own needs. "When you are disillusioned, afraid or feeling threatened or unsafe, it's hard to engage your kindness instinct. You can become exhausted, indifferent and uncaring—all states that cause you distress."

On the other hand, the more you can incorporate kindness into your life, the happier and better you'll feel. "Study after study shows the positive effect of kindness," Cousineau notes. Research by noted positive psychologist Barbara Fredrickson at the University of North Carolina shows that positive emotions can broaden and build our capacity to have joy and happiness in our lives. "You begin to develop an upward spiral of positive feelings, so it feels good to do good," Cousineau adds.

There's ample research to back this idea. In a recent study from the University of Zurich in Switzerland, participants were asked to either spend money on others or on themselves. The givers had higher levels of self-reported happiness compared to those who were not as generous. And in a survey of 4,582 adults, 68 percent of those who engaged in volunteer activities for two hours a week (about 100 hours a year) reported that it made them feel physically healthier, 92 percent said it enriched their sense of purpose, 89 percent said it improved their sense of well-being, 73 percent said it lowered stress and 77 percent felt it improved their emotional health. Other studies have shown that kindness can help improve symptoms related to depression, anxiety and social isolation in teens; improve body image; and strengthen romantic relationships.

Doing nice things for others can also effect real physical change. A 2013 study found that high school students who volunteered for an hour a week helping children in after-school programs had lower levels of inflammation and cholesterol and a lower body mass index after 10 weeks. And in another 2013 study of 1,100 adults, aged 51 to 91, those who volunteered an average of four hours a week were 40 percent less likely to develop hypertension than those who didn't dedicate any time to helping others or volunteering.

89%
OF PEOPLE SAY VOLUNTEERING 100 HOURS A YEAR IMPROVES THEIR SENSE OF WELL-BEING

Training for an endurance event that supports a good cause can yield big payoffs in positivity and mood.

WHAT DOES IT MEAN TO BE KIND?

"Kindness is love in action," notes Cousineau. "It's the embodiment of your feelings of warmth and generosity toward others and the world at large—and your desire to bring relief to those who are suffering. In this way, kindness is both a quality of loving presence and an orientation to life that is intentional and active."

In other words, if you want to experience the full benefits of kindness, there needs to be some intent behind your actions. Donating to a coworker who's doing a charity walk is helpful, but if you don't derive personal meaning from it, says Cousineau, you may not reap your own benefits. Signing up to walk yourself or helping your coworker prepare by training with her can deepen the experience.

"When we engage in activities that are kind both to ourselves and to others, we feel the full range of positive emotions, and that is what can make real changes in our physiology," she adds. "The more we do, the more it will ignite that caring circuitry in our brains."

CULTIVATING KINDNESS

Most of us want to believe we are kind and have the best intentions to live a compassionate life. But it can be difficult on a daily basis to keep up our emotional empathy. Cousineau suggests a few ways to integrate kindness that can have the biggest effect on your own state of happiness.

START LOCAL

"You don't have to fly down to help victims of a hurricane or earthquake. If you can help them financially, that's a good place to start, but is there also a way to be helpful right now?" asks Cousineau. Maybe that's asking an elderly neighbor if you can pick up her groceries. Or volunteering to spend an hour a week at the library shelving books or helping at your kids' school. "You don't have to be Mother Teresa to make a difference; even small things in your own neighborhood can have an impact," she adds.

LOVE YOURSELF

"Often you need to start being kind to yourself—it can help you be more resilient, so you can then be better able to help others," Cousineau says. That can mean anything from taking time to go to the gym to making sure you're eating healthfully and getting a good night's sleep. "These are all acts of self-kindness that we often neglect to do for ourselves," she adds.

73%
OF PEOPLE SAY VOLUNTEERING LOWERS STRESS LEVELS

SAY HI TO A STRANGER

"We tend to be tribal and mostly stick with the people we know or who may look like us," Cousineau says. You don't have to go up to a stranger on the street or subway—it can simply be a matter of introducing yourself to a new employee in your office at a meeting or striking up a conversation in line at the coffee bar.

BE GRATEFUL

There's ample research that shows counting your blessings makes you happier, but it can also make you kinder. "Practicing gratitude is powerful stuff," Cousineau says. "It makes you feel better, and you can often pass on that spark of positive feelings to those around you."

MAKE A SMALL TIME COMMITMENT

It doesn't take a lot to reap the benefits of volunteering—just a couple of hours a week can make a difference, both for yourself and for others. Your local religious community is often the perfect place to start, but there are plenty of other organizations that will be happy to have you help. "Find something that resonates with you personally," Cousineau suggests. "Think about what you would enjoy doing that will also help you derive some sort of meaning."

SEND A THANK-YOU

Most of us don't often put a pen to paper these days—it's far easier to fire off a text or e-mail. But sending a thank-you to someone who has done a kind act for you can make an impact on them, as well as on you, says Cousineau. And taking the time to write it out and mail it can make it that much more meaningful.

Taking part in positive acts like volunteering can broaden and build on your capacity for joy.

92%
OF PEOPLE REPORT THAT VOLUNTEERING ENRICHES THEIR SENSE OF PURPOSE

SOURCE "RX: IT'S GOOD TO BE GOOD 2017 COMMENTARY: PRESCRIBING VOLUNTEERISM FOR HEALTH, HAPPINESS, RESILIENCE, AND LONGEVITY," BY STEPHEN POST, PH.D., *AMERICAN JOURNAL OF HEALTH PROMOTION*

Volunteering just a couple of hours a week can yield big benefits.

10 WAYS TO BE KINDER

1
SMILE AT A STRANGER.

2
SAY "I LOVE YOU" TO SOMEONE YOU CARE ABOUT.

3
CLEAN UP THE DIRTY DISHES IN THE SINK (EVEN IF THEY'RE NOT YOURS!).

4
HOLD THE DOOR OPEN FOR SOMEONE.

5

COMPLIMENT SOMEONE FOR A POSITIVE ATTITUDE OR EFFORT.

6

PHONE A FRIEND INSTEAD OF JUST SENDING A TEXT.

7

DONATE TO A CAUSE YOU BELIEVE IN.

8

TALK TO A HOMELESS PERSON.

9

VOLUNTEER AT A SOUP KITCHEN OR FOOD BANK.

10

PICK UP SOME TRASH THAT YOU SEE ON THE STREET.

THE IMPORTANCE OF RESILIENCE

LIFE'S NOT ALWAYS PEACHES AND CREAM. LEARNING HOW TO BOUNCE BACK WHEN TIMES ARE TOUGH CAN HELP YOU ENJOY THE INEVITABLE ROLLER COASTER

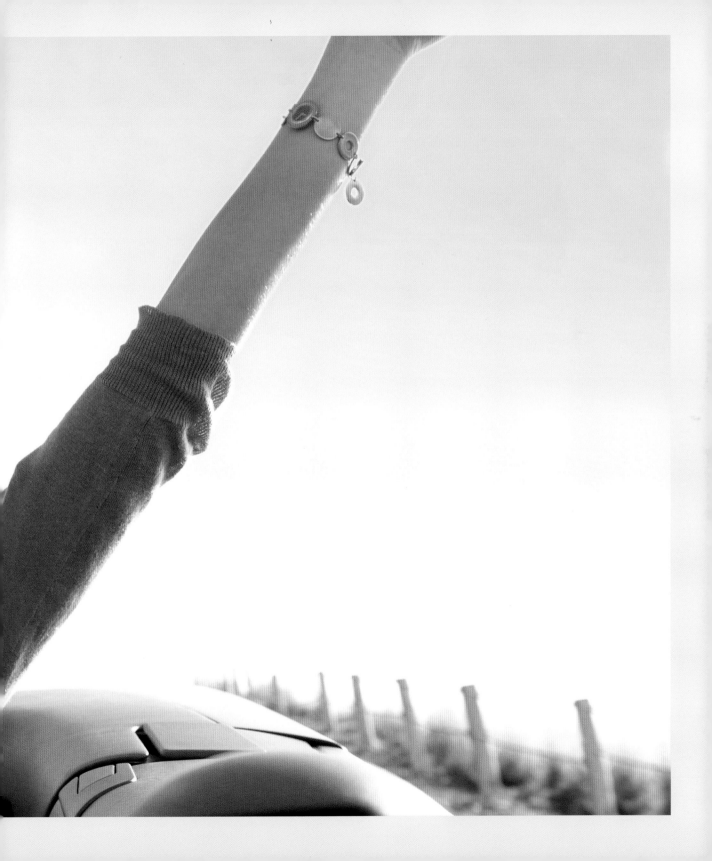

PURSUIT OF HAPPINESS

Turn to others for support who are or have been in your shoes.

→ **WE ALL KNOW SOMEONE** who seems bulletproof when it comes to life's challenges. In the face of adversity, they're able to bounce back quickly and with little damage. It's not that they are emotionless robots or have their head stuck in the sand. They're simply more resilient.

According to the American Psychological Association, resilience is "the process of adapting well in the face of adversity, trauma, tragedy, threats or significant sources of stress—such as family and relationship problems, serious health problems, or workplace and financial stressors." Basically, it's bending rather than breaking, says Steven Southwick, M.D., a professor of psychiatry at Yale School of Medicine and the National Center for Post-Traumatic Stress Disorder.

Research suggests that people who are more psychologically resilient have higher levels of emotional stability, dispositional gratitude, purpose in life and feelings of altruism. Although there isn't much data on resilience and happiness, experts say the two are likely related.

Luckily, resilience isn't something you either have or don't. "Anybody can learn to become more resilient," says Dr. Southwick, coauthor of *Resilience: The Science of Mastering Life's Greatest Challenges.* "Through different points in our lives, we are faced with some stress, sometimes traumatic. How we negotiate this stress has a big effect on our overall mental and physical well-being."

We don't always know when stress may strike, but we can be better prepared to meet it when it does. Try incorporating these tips to strengthen your resilience, and reap the benefits in good times as well as bad.

1

BUILD A STRONG SOCIAL NETWORK

Coping skills are helpful, but before you work on those, be sure you have a group of friends and family who are there for you. "The single most important thing is to have a strong, supportive community on whom you can rely and who can rely on you," says Suniya S. Luthar, Ph.D., professor of psychology at Arizona State University.

And we'll get farther in life by turning to others. "Remember we are social animals—none of us can live as an island," Luthar adds. "As strong or determined as you might be, you need a support system that catches you when you fall."

Being around people you can trust makes you more likely to use active coping techniques such as problem-solving, gathering information and attracting support rather than passive ones like avoidance or denial, Dr. Southwick adds. And in to be most effective, support needs to go two ways. "Giving support is just as health-promoting as receiving it," she says.

2

BE PHYSICALLY ACTIVE

Among the many benefits of exercise, here's one you may not have thought of—physical fitness is linked to resilience. According to a study published in the journal *Interface Focus,* both a regular workout regimen and weekend warrior-type spontaneous activity blunt stress, minimize inflammation and keep our brains healthy, all of which add up to increased resilience.

"Exercise is helpful for both physical and emotional resilience. It helps you respond in more adaptive ways," says Dr. Southwick. It doesn't matter if it's walking, running, swimming, playing golf or scuba diving—any type of movement can help.

3

CULTIVATE MINDFULNESS

Mindfulness practices such as meditation, breath work and yoga continue to be associated with more and more benefits, including resilience. In a 2016 study, Indian researchers found that undergraduate students with higher mindfulness had greater resilience and life satisfaction. "Mindful people...can better cope with difficult thoughts and emotions without becoming overwhelmed or shutting down," the study authors wrote.

"Mindfulness trains you to become an observer of your thoughts and emotions," Dr. Southwick adds. This allows you to decide when to engage your brain in any of those feelings and when to simply let them go by without judging.

4

FACE YOUR FEARS

We tend to avoid what makes us uncomfortable, but that rarely helps. "If you don't face your fears, it restricts your life and you never extinguish what is making you afraid," Dr. Southwick says.

He suggests thinking of fear as a friend. "Try to understand your fear and learn as much as you can about it," he says. See how you can view the fear as an opportunity to develop any specific skills that would help you face it.

For example, if you are afraid of public speaking and need to give a presentation, think about all the things that could go wrong and practice how you would handle each situation. Be prepared for questions that the audience may ask and how you will respond. It can be beneficial to practice in front of others or to record yourself.

5

FIND A SENSE OF PURPOSE

Having a well-defined purpose in life can not only lead to superior cognitive functioning, it can also make you more likely to be able to roll with the punches. Famed German philosopher Friedrich Nietzsche once said, "He who has a why to live for, can bear almost any how." People who are defending their mission or purpose in life tend to be more resilient than those who don't have such a mission. "We certainly saw that with many people we interviewed. If you are fighting for something you believe in, you can be pretty darn strong," Dr. Southwick explains. According to a study of 2,157 military veterans in the *Journal of Psychiatric Research*, a stronger sense of purpose in life may promote resilience.

How can you reap the benefits of this finding? Develop a positive outlook for your future. Try creating a vision board to help you achieve your goals. Living with purpose will afford you a better understanding of why certain things happen, and you'll be better equipped to handle what comes your way.

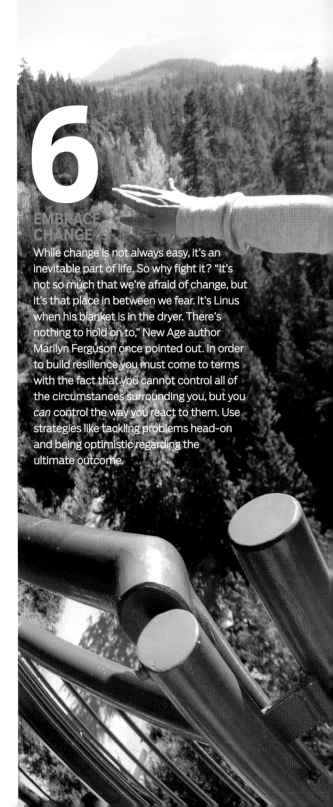

6

EMBRACE CHANGE

While change is not always easy, it's an inevitable part of life. So why fight it? "It's not so much that we're afraid of change, but it's that place in between we fear. It's Linus when his blanket is in the dryer. There's nothing to hold on to," New Age author Marilyn Ferguson once pointed out. In order to build resilience you must come to terms with the fact that you cannot control all of the circumstances surrounding you, but you *can* control the way you react to them. Use strategies like tackling problems head-on and being optimistic regarding the ultimate outcome.

Doing
something
that scares
you helps
you grow.

STAYING POSITIVE

FRIENDS, FAMILY OR WORK RAINING ON YOUR PARADE? EXPERTS SHARE HOW TO SPREAD SOME SUNSHINE WHEN THESE SIX COMMON GLOOM-AND-DOOMERS COME YOUR WAY

→ **MOST OF THE TIME YOU** like to think of yourself as a pretty positive person, capable of seeing the glass as half full, not half empty, and trying to help those around you see the bright side of things, too. But every now and then you're hit with a deluge of negativity, whether it's coming from your partner, friend, boss or family (usually someone you just can't walk away from!). We may love these naysayers, but their attitudes can be a total downer. What's an upbeat person to do with these saboteurs? We talked to relationship experts to learn how to handle the black clouds that regularly cross your path while keeping your own outlook as sunny as possible.

BLACK CLOUD

YOUR PARTNER CONSTANTLY STRESSES ABOUT MONEY

Financial concerns can create conflict in any relationship, especially a romantic one. "Try to take these worries away from the partner, and instill a ray of sunshine in this situation," suggests Carrie Cole, M.Ed., L.P.C.-S., a therapist at The Gottman Institute Center for Relationship Wellness. It may be productive to be empathetic with your partner, suggests Cole. Identify the emotion in his or her negative statements. Say something like, "It seems like you feel hopeless about the situation" or "You seem so disappointed that there's not as much money as you hoped there would be by now. What's the worst part in that for you?" Acknowledge your partner's feelings and stay focused on him or her. You might ask "What does this mean to you that there isn't enough money?" or "How would having more money improve things for you?" "When we define emotions, it sort of shrinks them down to size," Cole says.

If you and your partner are arguing frequently, whether it's over money, responsibilities or other factors in the relationship, remind him or her that you need to feel successful in the union, advises Cole. "Consider saying 'I need to hear some appreciation for what I am doing in this relationship,'" she suggests.

There's also a tendency for nitpickers to speak a lot in the abstract, says Errol A. Gibbs, coauthor of *Discovering Your Optimum "Happiness Index" (OHI)*, with his wife of 40 years, Marjorie G. Gibbs. "The way to slow down someone who's sabotaging is to bring facts to the conversation to get them thinking," Gibbs adds. When your partner exclaims "We're broke!" or "We'll never be able to pay off debt!" those are emotional statements, says Gibbs. Try looking over your finances together and getting a clear sense of what the situation actually is. This way, you can have discussions based on facts

31%

NUMBER OF ADULTS WITH PARTNERS WHO REPORT THAT MONEY IS A MAJOR SOURCE OF CONFLICT IN THEIR RELATIONSHIP.

SOURCE AMERICAN PSYCHOLOGICAL ASSOCIATION "STRESS IN AMERICA" 2014 SURVEY

Empathize with a friend who is down but also help her take action for herself.

and information instead of emotions like fear. "By bringing facts to the conversation, you're able to better explore opportunities to assess the situation," Gibbs suggests. Once you have facts in front of you, discuss a solution, like putting a budget together or coming up with a plan to pay off debt, he advises.

BLACK CLOUD

YOUR FRIEND IS ALWAYS DOWN IN THE DUMPS

Some of us have that friend we've known for decades whom we love, but when we see their name pop up on caller ID, we think "Oh no, what now?" or "I can't handle their drama today." Then, you might feel guilty, like you're a bad friend.

Try to keep in mind that this type of person is coming to you because she values you, says Gibbs. He suggests setting boundaries with your friend about how long you have to talk to her, or waiting to call her back at a time that's better for you, when you're in a good frame of mind and relaxed and ready to help.

And when that friend goes down that rabbit hole of all the things that are going wrong in her life right now, you can empathize and say something like "I'm sorry that this is a very difficult time for you," suggests Cole. You could also ask, "What would it take to make things better for you?" and then "How can we form a plan to take some action and make things better?" "Try to get them to problem-solve for themselves," says Cole. When you suggest something like "Why don't you try to do this?" friends like these may simply shoot holes in your ideas and strategies, and often you end up feeling worse, because you've already invested time and energy, and everything you're suggesting to help gets shot down or sabotaged in some way, says Cole. Helping them figure it out for themselves takes you out of the middle.

This is also another place to reflect back to the person what they're feeling, adds Cole. You might want to say, "It sounds like you're very disappointed about that" or "It sounds like you're very sad" or "It sounds like you're depressed." You might also follow this up with a statement like "I wish that I had the tools and the skills to help you through that, but I don't. I would suggest that you talk to somebody who does. There are many qualified therapists. Would you consider reaching out to one of them?"

And at some point, tell the friend "I've really enjoyed hearing from you; however, I need to go now," says Cole. Then make sure you take a break for yourself—and build your own happiness reserves back up.

BLACK CLOUD

YOUR FATHER SEES THE DARK SIDE OF EVERY SITUATION

Parents can be great at inserting themselves into how their own children run their lives, including how they raise their children, fix their homes and manage their finances. You might have a visiting father or in-law who points out the overgrown shrubbery, the leaky faucet in the bathroom, as well as all the traffic in your neighborhood and how their home or community is far superior. While this might just be that person's way of communicating, it can grind on even the happiest person's last nerve.

"There are times when someone is really trying to be helpful, but they just don't know any better, and they might actually use language that isn't optimal for your happiness," says Melanie Rudd, Ph.D., an assistant professor of marketing at the University of Houston's C. T. Bauer College of Business. Rudd and her colleagues recently submitted research to the *Journal of Consumer Research* about how our cultural background can influence our mindset to be optimistic about recovery when facing a health challenge. "Remember that advice is often well-meant...and sometimes it's a nice idiom, but it's not going to be optimal for you," Rudd says. Her team's latest research found that some people are more optimistic when they prepare for a difficult situation by imagining ahead of time what they'll do when faced with that challenge. Try to prepare for your father's visit by doing a meditation that day, having some time to yourself, and telling yourself that you'll be calm and collected no matter what he says. Remind yourself, "He's trying to be helpful." Other people might find they would handle a situation better by responding to it with behaviors and activities in the moment. You might tell yourself that you'll get up and clear dishes when your father starts picking on something. Or prepare to thank him and change the subject: "Thanks for your advice, Dad. Can I get you a drink or dessert?"

BLACK CLOUD
YOUR BOSS IS CONSTANTLY ON YOUR CASE

If you feel like your boss is sucking the happiness right out of your soul, you probably find your workplace a tough place to spend your time. And while you can't avoid this happiness saboteur—unless you're willing to change jobs—you can try to reframe your employer's nitpicking as "constructive criticism." When a boss is nitpicking, he or she might be doing that because of your work speed or the quality of what you're producing. "You can always go back to the boss and ask for more specifics about your role. Say, 'Please share a few steps that I can do to improve my performance' or 'Can you give me some tools that would help?'" says Gibbs. Look internally at the work you are doing and try to understand what the requirements are in the context of your job.

Keep in mind that while you think you boss is harping at you because she doesn't like you or she's in a particularly bad mood, problems could be coming from pressure above, like from her bosses, or a status report, says Gibbs. "Try to change your attitude at work," he suggests. "Engage in a discussion with your boss and look for common ground."

40%
PERCENTAGE OF AMERICANS WHO REPORT THEIR JOB IS VERY OR EXTREMELY STRESSFUL.
SOURCE AMERICAN INSTITUTE OF STRESS REPORT

BLACK CLOUD
YOUR COLLEAGUE WON'T STOP COMPLAINING

All of us have probably experienced a whining coworker at times. It's normal to gripe about work occasionally, but there comes a point when those moanings feel like they'll never end and you dread being anywhere near that coworker or even going to work. Nip the colleague's complaints in the bud by not commiserating with them. "Say, 'I'm sorry you're struggling with that. I would love to be supportive of you, but I'm probably not the best person to talk to. I don't have the tools or skills to help you through your particular situation. Perhaps it might be better if you went and spoke to somebody who did," Cole suggests. While that might sound a bit formal, you're letting them know that you don't want to hear their negativity and that they'll have to find someone else to yammer to if they want support.

BLACK CLOUD
YOUR MOM NITPICKS ABOUT YOUR WEIGHT

Many of us can relate to a loved one making a comment about a new hairstyle we've tried, something we're wearing or whether we've put on a few pounds. Family members seem to know how to home in on our most sensitive touch points and press directly on those buttons. If you know you'll be in a social situation with a relative who harangues you about a sensitive subject, like your appearance, prep yourself with some positive self-talk beforehand. And have some phrases to tell yourself that can help you guard against the other person's negativity. "If they don't like the way I look or the way I dress or whatever, whose opinion of me matters more, mine or theirs? I'm doing the best I can with what I have to work with right now, and I don't need to let other people define me. I can define myself," says Cole. And limit the time you spend with anyone who focuses on your flaws.

In addition, it's important to focus on self-care, Cole adds. When you feel tensions rise with a family member, partner or child, it might serve you well to put yourself in "time-out" to take a break, go on a walk or do something that soothes you. "Make sure you say something like, 'I'm not leaving you or this conversation, but I need to take care of myself for a few minutes,'" suggests Cole. "Let the person know how long you'll be gone and when you'll be back so that they don't feel anxiety about your leaving."

And finally, have some empathy for whoever might be throwing you some shade. "Try not to think of people as saboteurs," says Gibbs. "They may be seeking attention or validation for their own inadequacies." He suggests maintaining a relaxed disposition about your situation. If you can muster the patience, consider asking questions of the saboteur, like "What would you do if you were me in this situation?" Make the person the expert, suggests Gibbs, so he will ultimately give you some space or see things from your point of view.

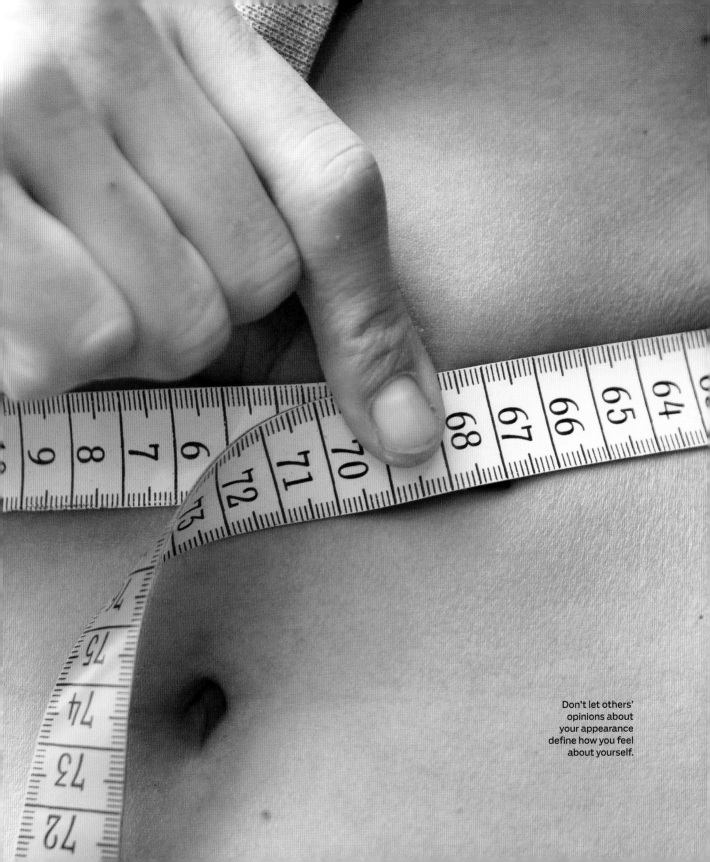

Don't let others' opinions about your appearance define how you feel about yourself.

Mutual support mixed with independence is key to marital happiness.

THE HAPPINESS CONUNDRUM

WHAT HAPPENS WHEN THE THINGS YOU THOUGHT WOULD MAKE YOU DELIGHTED ARE NOW CAUSING YOU DISTRESS? TOP EXPERTS REVEAL HOW TO TURN THINGS AROUND

→ **THERE'S A STUDY** from the late 1970s that examined the happiness levels of lottery winners and found that after a few months recent winners reported their levels of everyday pleasure were actually lower than those of people who were recent victims of catastrophic accidents and were left paraplegic or quadriplegic. The bottom line? The things you believe will make you happy can actually cause the most displeasure. Experts call this the happiness conundrum. From landing the perfect job to marrying the ideal partner, we often start out thinking certain milestones will make us satisfied, but instead they cause suffering. Recognize yourself in this scenario? Here's what you can do to decrease your displeasure and increase your sense of well-being.

THE CONUNDRUM

"I'll be happy if...I get married."

■ More than 90 percent of people in Western cultures marry by age 50—but then again, more than 40 percent of married couples in the U.S. eventually divorce, according to the American Psychological Association. Of course, no relationship is perfect, and if you ask 10 people for their secrets to a great marriage, you're likely to get 10 different answers. But there are a few underlying themes about what can help sustain a happy marriage.

YOUR HAPPINESS PLAN

Maintain your own identity It's important to build on shared intimacy, but at the same time it's also crucial to set some boundaries and protect your autonomy. "I think it's essential to pay attention to your own needs," says Laura Doyle, author of several books about marriage, including *The Empowered Wife*. "I try to do at least three things a day for my own happiness, even if that's something frivolous like singing at the top of my lungs, taking a hot bath or meeting a friend for coffee. It makes me feel good, and that's who I need to be in order to have a good relationship."

Offer support without control One of the keys to a happy marriage is to nurture and comfort each other and satisfy each partner's needs for dependency while offering encouragement and support, according to Judith S. Wallerstein, Ph.D., author of *The Good Marriage: How and Why Love Lasts*. But that can also mean laying off the criticism, adds Doyle. "I was under the impression that I could change my husband if I could control

him, but the more I would criticize, the harder it would be for us to stay connected." Have open conversations instead, she adds, and focus more on the outcome that you want than what's not being done to your liking.

Fight clean All marriages involve some level of disagreements, but destructive fighting styles can be particularly damaging. Yelling, criticizing or withdrawing from the discussion are likelier to lead to breakups than constructive strategies such as finding out what your partner is feeling, listening to their viewpoint, or trying to make them laugh, according to a study in *Journal of Marriage and Family*.

THE CONUNDRUM

"I'll be happy if...I have a baby."

■ Women, especially, often espouse the idea that they will only find fulfillment if

Oh, baby! Caring for a child also means giving yourself a respite.

they start a family. And having children can truly be one of the most incredibly satisfying and life-enhancing experiences we can have. But a study published in 2016 in the *American Journal of Sociology* found that parents in the U.S. were on average 12 percent unhappier than those without kids, creating a "parenting happiness gap."

Financial concerns and work stress often tie into this level of unhappiness, as do high expectations about child-rearing. But often it's the primary caregiver (which in the U.S. is typically the mother) who feels the most stress and dissatisfaction with the day-in, day-out responsibilities of parenting. "It doesn't matter if you are a stay-at-home parent or a working one, many of us end up feeling guilty and unfulfilled," notes Randi Zinn, the author of *Going Beyond Mom: How to Activate Your Mind, Body & Business After Baby.* "Our culture puts an inordinate amount of pressure on us to do everything, and it can be very debilitating."

YOUR HAPPINESS PLAN

Take some time for yourself This is especially crucial in some of the early days of being a parent, Zinn says. That's exactly when you need to invest in some self-care, and one of the best ways to do that is to incorporate more movement into your day. "You don't have to be at the gym or in a group cycling class—just get up and get the blood moving, even if that's walking with the stroller around the neighborhood or getting on the floor and doing some stretches," Zinn suggests. "Even if you only have five minutes and can't leave the house, use it to your advantage—you'll have a greater sense of control over your body and what it can do." (Caveat: Make sure your doctor signs off on exercise before you start any formal physical activity.)

Be more mindful "Having a baby is a massive life change, but incorporating some tools of mindfulness can help you navigate this change," Zinn says. "It allows you to slow down some of your thoughts when possible and be an observer of your own reactions." Again, it

doesn't take a lot of time, she adds. Whether you're nursing, snuggling or just washing the dishes, use that time to breathe and be present. "Breathe evenly, allowing your body to relax and taking in all the sensations that you are feeling. Think about how you want to feel—peaceful, happy and content," she advises.

Work with your partner There's a lot going on in your household when a new baby joins the party, so communication is key, says Zinn. Try to carve out some time for you and your partner to check in with each other regularly. "Some people like to have 'couch talk' time, where at least once a week they sit down and discuss what's going on in their lives and with each other," she says. These communication patterns can be essential in sharing what your needs and expectations are, or for simply talking about your day and your experiences.

Make new friends We're social creatures by nature, and having this sense of community is especially important for new parents. Whether you're sharing secrets of sleep training or trying to figure out how to handle an intrusive in-law, establishing relationships with others in similar situations can be crucial to your happiness. "Most of us don't live in a village like our ancestors or have multiple generations of help in the same house, so we need that community to turn to for advice and support," says Zinn. Find a play group, sign up for a class or even go online and click on to a new parent

PARENTS IN THE U.S. WERE 12 PERCENT UNHAPPIER THAN THOSE WITHOUT KIDS, CREATING A "PARENTING HAPPINESS GAP."

Kids making you crazy? Take a time-out for yourself every now and then.

forum to ask questions. And don't be afraid to reach out to other women who might be able to share ideas outside of parenthood, whether you want to discuss going back to work or even starting your own business.

THE CONUNDRUM

"I'll be happy if...I land a perfect job."

■ Are you doing what you once dreamed would make you happy? Whether it's pulling down a high salary, working in a so-called glamorous field or having the opportunity to travel the world, jobs you might have once strived for may in reality be making you miserable. From having long hours and repetitive tasks to a nightmarish boss, work can be one of the biggest triggers of unhappiness in our lives. Here's how to make it better.

YOUR HAPPINESS PLAN

Take time to disconnect Technology makes it easy to be on top of work, but an overload of information may be making you miserable. "You have to learn how to unplug from your job for at least a short time every day," notes Margaret Greenberg, a positive psychologist and the coauthor of *Profit From the Positive*. That's easier said than done in our 24-7 information age, but your brain needs a break. Taking time off will help you connect with those around you and also give you a chance to recharge so you're ready to take on the challenges that the workplace may throw at you.

Interview yourself A job that once might have seemed perfect is now keeping you up at night. Where did it go wrong? "See if you can identify when things shifted for you," advises Victor Shamas, Ph.D., author of *Deep Creativity* and a

> **UNPLUG FROM YOUR JOB FOR AT LEAST A SHORT TIME EVERY DAY—YOUR BRAIN NEEDS A BREAK, AND YOU NEED TIME TO CONNECT WITH THOSE CLOSE TO YOU.**

former professor of psychology at the University of Arizona. "If you find your current situation uninspiring, unfulfilling or unenjoyable, ask yourself how much of it is the situation and how much is you." If your response is more about your attitude than your employer, you can take steps to change your outlook. But if the answer is situational, you may have a decision to make. "Can I change the culture and the conditions of my job? If you can, great, and if you can't, it may be time to make a change," says Shamas.

Focus on the positive Are you going through a tough time at work? Think of it as an opportunity to build resilience. "Failures and setbacks are normal aspects of all careers," Greenberg notes. "Viewing them as learning opportunities can help you bounce back so you can try again." And put things in perspective: "Apply a 'Me-Always-Everything' framework," says Greenberg. Was the problem entirely your fault? Do these issues always happen to you? Are setbacks normal in every aspect of your life? "The answer to all of these is probably no," she maintains. "That helps give you a sense of where your challenge may exist."

Try to view
work setbacks
as learning
opportunities.

HOW TO RAISE JOYFUL KIDS

THERE ARE STEPS YOU CAN TAKE TO MAKE SURE YOUR CHILDREN ALWAYS LOOK ON THE SUNNY SIDE

→ **DID YOU KNOW THAT** happiness can be learned? "Think of happiness as a set of skills rather than an inborn personality trait," Christine Carter, the author of *Raising Happiness: 10 Simple Steps for More Joyful Kids and Happier Parents,* has said. Of course, some children have a more cheerful disposition; others are a little grouchier. But she encourages parents to consider happiness to be like learning a language: "Some kids are going to be good at picking it up quickly, others are going to struggle. But we all need to be taught the basic grammar. And we all need to practice that grammar to become fluent."

TEACH KINDNESS

Often kids focus on their own needs rather than on helping others, but in the long run that won't make them happy. "We think that happiness comes about because you get things for yourself," according to Richard Ryan, a psychologist at the University of Rochester. But "it turns out that…giving gets you more," he adds. According to a study, the more people participated in meaningful activities, like helping others, the happier they were. Harvard psychologist Richard Weissbourd has offered the following recommendations for raising kind children: Make caring for others a priority by stressing kindness over happiness, provide opportunities for children to practice caring and gratitude, expand your child's circle of concern to more than just small group of friends and family and be a strong moral role model, leading by example.

ENCOURAGE OPTIMISM

Helping your child to look on the bright side can make navigating the tough teen years easier. Australian researchers found the more optimistic a group of 12- to 13-year-olds were, the less likely they were to become depressed. But even if your kid isn't naturally positive, he or she can learn to be. When a problem arises, encourage your child to recognize the issue and think about what caused it, as well as how he or she could improve the situation, Martin Seligman, director of the Positive Psychology Center at the University of Pennsylvania, has reported. Also, keep in mind that your child will pick up on your positive outlook, so rather than complaining that the line in the grocery store is too long, try saying, "This line is moving so fast, we'll be out of here in no time!"

DON'T PUSH PERFECTIONISM

Encouraging your child to do his or her best is one thing; focusing on it to the exception of everything else is another. Psychologists say it's more important to praise children for their effort and hard work than for their intelligence or skill. Research by Stanford University psychologist Caroline Dweck has found that when children were praised for their intelligence in solving a puzzle, they were less willing to take on a harder task; those who were given positive feedback for working hard most often opted to attempt a more challenging task.

"They feel smart when they are working on something really difficult and making progress," says Dweck. And realizing that it's normal to not always be perfect is an essential skill to achieving happiness. "We need to teach children that it is totally okay to make mistakes—we often learn life's best lessons when we make mistakes," Carter has said. "Sometimes a B+ is a cause for celebration."

BOLSTER WILLPOWER

One of the biggest signs of future success is self-discipline—the ability to delay gratification. A well-known study looked at how preschoolers reacted if they were given the choice to eat one marshmallow immediately or two if they waited 15

Celebrate your victories together, whether big or small.

minutes. Those who were able to wait out the time and get twice the reward statistically had a higher level of success and happiness decades later. Researchers say you can help your children develop more willpower by focusing on the reward ahead or distracting them by focusing on something else. Learning self-discipline can also help kids better handle frustration and stress.

KEEP UP YOUR OWN POSITIVITY

Studies show that depression among parents (especially moms) can significantly impact children at all ages. A research roundup published in *Pediatrics and Child Health* found maternal depression can make it

"[CHILDREN] FEEL SMART WHEN THEY ARE WORKING ON SOMETHING REALLY DIFFICULT AND MAKING PROGRESS."

—PSYCHOLOGIST CAROLINE DWECK

difficult for newborns to bond, which could lead them to become more anxious or angrier and develop cognitive difficulties. Toddlers and preschoolers who have a depressed parent may be more aggressive and destructive, and less likely to engage in creative play. And school-age children of depressed mothers are at a higher risk of depression and anxiety disorders, as well as ADHD (attention deficit hyperactivity disorder). If you feel like you may be suffering from even mild depression, it's important to get help (for more details, see "When It's More Than Just Sadness," page 35). Remember that kids are very resilient, and any action you take to help yourself will also help them. The happier you are, the happier your children will be.

Teach your kids the skills of building happiness at a young age.

"WE NEED TO TEACH CHILDREN THAT IT IS TOTALLY OKAY TO MAKE MISTAKES."
— AUTHOR CHRISTINE CARTER

EASY FIXES FOR CHEERFUL CHILDREN

IT'S NOT AS DAUNTING A TASK AS IT MAY SEEM. HERE, A FEW SIMPLE WAYS TO HELP YOUR LITTLE ONES THRIVE

DO

allow your children some downtime, because less stress equals happier kids.

DON'T

be a tiger mom, pushing your kids to succeed at all costs.

DO

make some "me time." A happy mom leads to happy kids. So go ahead—schedule that manicure!

DON'T

devote every minute you have to your children, no matter how much they want you to.

DO

encourage quality time with dad. Studies reveal that feeling loved by dad is more important for a child's happiness than feeling love from mom.

DON'T

limit child-rearing responsibilities to the mother like it's the 1950s. Whenever possible, kids need time with their mom and dad!

 DO

customize your parenting approach to your child's personality. Some children need more structure, while others flourish with greater autonomy.

DON'T

use a one-size-fits-all approach to parenting, because each child is different.

 DO

draw boundaries. Kids thrive on routine, so stick to your guns and enforce that bedtime!

DON'T

try to be your child's best friend, as tempting as it may be.

 DO

relish the mess. Too often we miss moments of joy because we are distracted by small things like a sink full of dishes.

DON'T

be a neat freak, forgoing fun and quality time for a bunch of daily chores.

FIND YOUR HAPPY PLACE

THEY SAY THAT LOCATION IS EVERYTHING. IF YOUR HOMETOWN ISN'T WHERE YOU WANT TO BE, HERE'S HOW TO FIND THE RIGHT FIT—EVEN IF IT'S JUST AROUND THE CORNER!

→ **WHEN I THINK BACK** to this year, I will forever remember it as the time I found my home. When I say the word "home," sure, I'm talking about a physical structure—in my case, a cabin-like condo in the Mount Tabor neighborhood of Portland, Oregon.

But when I think "home," I'm really talking about something deeper: a place where I finally feel like I belong. Where I've found my community, my tribe.

I moved to Portland nearly 20 years ago after a dramatic breakup. Heartbroken, three days before the eve of the new millennium, I sat on my rooftop in Brooklyn, looking out over the cityscape—the World Trade Center to the left, the Empire State Building straight ahead. I was 30, freshly single, and after eight years in NYC, I was ready for a change. I'd always felt drawn to the city of Portland, which I'd originally visited on a postcollege road trip: I loved that it was an outdoorsy city with a small-town feel, and I made a promise to myself that night in New York to move there. I made good on my resolution, and moved to Portland in September 2000.

And things were good for a while. I joined a running group, explored the city and was wowed by the relatively cheap rent, laid-back quality of life and friendly vibe. It proved to be truly the oasis that I'd imagined on that lonely night in December 1999: an eclectic, outdoorsy town that offered everything I had ever wanted in a city without a lot of hassle.

But that was before. Before the *Portlandia* TV show, before *The New York Times* fell in love with Portland, before the hipster invasion. Slowly but surely, my Little Town That Could was starting to experience growing pains. Traffic. Construction. Historic buildings destroyed for shiny new condos. Rent hikes and displacement.

It plummeted me into a soul-searching period where I found myself craving what I had originally sought—and found—in Portland in the first place: an outdoorsy, small-town feel. I debated moving to Ann Arbor, Michigan—close to my childhood hometown, filled with high school friends and family. But was I just nostalgic for a community that didn't exist anymore, and after having been gone from the Midwest for so long, could I ever go home again? I thought about the Oregon

> **"I COULDN'T OVERLOOK THAT I HAD ESTABLISHED DEEP ROOTS HERE. DID I REALLY WANT TO START ALL OVER AGAIN?"**

THE TOP 10 HAPPIEST CITIES IN THE UNITED STATES

1 BOULDER, CO

2 SANTA CRUZ/WATSONVILLE, CA

3 CHARLOTTESVILLE, VA

4 FORT COLLINS, CO

5 SAN LUIS OBISPO/PASO ROBLES/ ARROYO GRANDE, CA

6 SAN JOSE/SUNNYVALE/SANTA CLARA, CA

7 PROVO/OREM, UT

8 BRIDGEPORT/STAMFORD/NORWALK, CT

9 BARNSTABLE, MA

10 ANCHORAGE, AK

SOURCE *THE BLUE ZONES OF HAPPINESS: LESSONS FROM THE WORLD'S HAPPIEST PEOPLE,* BY DAN BUETTNER

Location and environment are two key attributes of a happy home.

Having family in the area can make any home feel cozier.

coast or Missoula, Montana, but the idea of reestablishing myself in a new town again was daunting. Despite my reservations, I couldn't overlook that I had established deep roots here. Did I really want to start all over again?

It turns out, my answer was right around the corner in a community called Montavilla, five miles from downtown. Named for being a village on the side of a mountain (the "mountain," in this case, is the 600-foot extinct volcano overlooking the city), it has everything I want in its cute six-block "downtown": a yoga studio, coffee shops, wine bars, restaurants and a movie theater. It's a place where you can walk down the street and feel like you're a part of a small town.

The other day, I hiked to the top of Mount Tabor, climbing the steep *Rocky*-like steps that are a popular exercise spot for Portlandians, to witness the view of Mount Hood on one side and the city on the other. Then I stopped for coffee, chatting with the barista before visiting the farmer's market, laughing with Katie the farmer, for whose lettuce I have developed an obsession. On my way home, I stopped in at the brewpub and chatted with my neighbors Bob and Martha and the brewery owner, Mike, before heading home to sit under the tree on my outdoor patio.

I have found my Shangri-la yet again, and I only had to change one number on my zip code to do it.

It's been 10 months now since I moved into my new home, and I'm happy each morning that I wake up to still be in the city that I love. It feels like I belong here more than ever. It took a lot of soul-searching and faith at times, but I can say I have finally found my dream place. So can you.

—*Megan McMorris*

THERE'S NO PLACE LIKE HOME

FEELING LIKE YOU HAVE ONE FOOT OUT THE DOOR?
HERE'S HOW TO DECIDE WHETHER
TO MAKE THE LEAP—AND WHERE TO GO

DETERMINE YOUR DIRECTION

"The first thing to do when contemplating a move is to look within," says Aida Vazin, M.A., a therapist in Newport Beach, California. "Ask yourself whether you're running away from something or towards something." They say "Wherever you go, there you are," and you don't want to move to a new town only to discover that your problems have followed you, Vazin adds. Make sure you're clearing up any unresolved issues before making a move. Write down what's causing you to look elsewhere. Are you dissatisfied with job opportunities? Growing tired of your circle of friends? Do you feel like you're just in a rut? Be honest about whether you'll really find what you're looking for in a different location or whether the thing you need to change instead is, in fact, your mindset.

NOTICE YOUR THOUGHT PATTERNS

If you dream about the desert because you're tired of shoveling snow or you've felt drawn toward a big city and don't know why, take note. "Go to your end goal and work back. If you're always feeling a pull toward Arizona, for example, ask yourself why. It can help you tease out your value systems," Vazin says.

THINK LOCALLY

Let's face it: We often take for granted what's right under our nose. "Are you really using your current city to your advantage?" says Florida-based psychologist Bart Rossi, Ph.D. "If you feel your city lacks a music or art scene and that's important to you, make sure you're exploring all the opportunities available to you. It could be that you just need a new perspective on where you are."

DO YOUR RESEARCH

Stymied about where you might best fit in? Start narrowing down your options with online quizzes and resources like livability.com, bestplaces.net or teleport.org, which are designed to help you find your sweet spot.

READY TO MAKE THE MOVE?

HELP ENSURE IT'S THE RIGHT ONE WITH THESE SIMPLE STRATEGIES

DO TAKE 5

"If you're feeling a pull toward a location, make a plan to visit for a few days, up to a week," suggests psychologist Bart Rossi, Ph.D. Instead of reserving a hotel downtown, book an Airbnb in a neighborhood to get a true feel for the vibe.

DON'T BE SHY

Moving to a new area will require getting out of your comfort zone, so be open to trying new things, whatever that may mean to you. "Now's the time to explore your true limitations, so make an adventure out of it," says therapist Aida Vazin.

Know what direction to take before you put down new roots.

DO BELLY UP TO THE BAR
Forget guidebooks: The best way to get a feel for a new place is to visit the local establishments. "Those who work in the hospitality industry are sometimes the best tour guides—they have their finger on the pulse of the city," Vazin says.

DON'T BE A STRANGER
The biggest factor that will determine your success in a new town is you. "Make a plan to take advantage of your location," says Rossi. Whether it's a networking event or finding a yoga studio, make a list of things you want to do in your first month.

DO HAVE AN OPEN MIND
"When you're new in a community, there are always going to be new norms to get used to," Vazin says. "Be patient, have an open mind and heart, and don't be surprised if it takes you six months to adjust to a new surrounding."

PART 3

CULTIVATING YOUR BLISS
SIMPLE WAYS TO FEEL FULFILLED

BEAT THE MONDAY BLAHS

START YOUR WORKWEEK WITH A POSITIVE MINDSET THANKS TO THESE SUREFIRE BAD-MOOD–BUSTING STRATEGIES

THE PLACE
Your bedroom

TIME
Early a.m.

THE SCENE
You're snuggled deep under your comforter. The alarm goes off. You reach over to shut off the music, but not before an intense sense of dread washes over you as you suddenly realize: **It's Monday.**

→ **IF THE SCENE ABOVE** rings true to you, you might be among the many who experience what psychologists colloquially call "the Monday blahs." It's an increasingly common feeling of discontent at the start of the workweek when you suddenly realize your weekend leisure time has come to a close and you've got at least a handful of days ahead where your free time is suddenly much more limited.

The good news is that it's not too difficult to break out of the blahs and take on whatever the day may bring. Start by following some of these simple expert-approved strategies.

START ON SUNDAY

Cut off the Monday blues by taking action the night before, advises Margaret Greenberg, a positive psychologist and author of *Profit from the Positive*. "I'm a big believer in establishing rituals," says Greenberg. Try taking a hot bath, laying out the clothes you want to wear, packing up a healthy lunch or doing whatever you need to get yourself in the right frame of mind. "Have an established pattern of things you do to get yourself ready for the week ahead," she says.

THINK POSITIVE

"A lot of what you feel when you're approaching a new week has to do with your perspective. If you're excited or you're anticipating something positive for the week, your Monday will start off a whole lot happier," notes Stacy Kaiser, a licensed psychotherapist and lifestyle coach based in Southern California. "But if you come in thinking that you've got nothing good going on but five whole days until the weekend, your whole outlook will skew and feel negative."

SET AN INTENTION

Before you roll out of bed on Monday, find a word or two that will help you determine your mindset for the day, Greenberg advises. Maybe it's "Help someone" or "Be patient." Then come back to this phrase whenever you find yourself needing a boost. "When you can set a positive intention for the day, you'll put yourself in a better state of mind," she adds.

START OFF EASY

Got a task you can't stand? Shuffle it to later in the day or even the week. "Be merciful on yourself," says Victor Shamas, a former psychology professor at the University of Arizona. "I'll do at least a couple of tasks that I enjoy before jumping into the other stuff."

> **"THINK ABOUT THE TRUE MEANING AND PURPOSE OF YOUR WORK... WHAT DID YOU ACCOMPLISH THAT MADE YOU FEEL PROUD?"**
> —PSYCHOLOGIST JOANNA BRANDI

CELEBRATE THE GOOD

Focus on what you like about your job. Maybe it's the people you work with, or that great new lunch place near your office. "Look at the whole picture—there's probably something there to feel good about," says Kaiser.

TREAT YOURSELF

"Create some satisfiers that you can insert throughout the week and make it that much better," Kaiser suggests. Monday might be the day you eat your favorite dinner or get that specialty drink you love at the coffee bar. Or save your Netflix binge for when you get home. "Put something you know you enjoy into your Monday so you have that to look forward to," she adds. You can also schedule something special, like lunch with your friend, in the middle of the week (hump day) so you have something to work toward.

VISUALIZE THE FUN

"You'll often hear people who want to lose weight cut out a picture of a favorite dress or outfit as motivation to help them reach their goals," says Kaiser. Try that same approach with work: Print out something symbolic of the coming weekend for you to look forward to, whether that's a movie premiere or a day at the beach. "This can be a distraction that can help you easily remind yourself why you want to get through your week," she adds.

REVIEW YOUR SUCCESS

At the end of your workweek, take a few moments and think about what went right, advises JoAnna Brandi, an executive coach and positive psychologist at ReturnOnHappiness.com. "Make a short entry in a journal about when you had some pleasure at work. Maybe it was when you were wholeheartedly engaged in something or you felt connected to certain people, even if it was a small interaction," she says. "Then take a deep breath and think about the true meaning and purpose of your work. How does it serve others? What did you accomplish that made you feel proud?" After you do this, she adds, savor the positive feelings, which can put you into the weekend feeling good and hopefully carry over to Monday as well.

DECORATE YOUR DESK

Aim to make your work space as pleasant as possible. Add some greenery: Research shows that having a plant nearby can make people feel less stress. Or hang up photos of your family or a vacation place you're either dying to go to or want to revisit.

CLEAN UP

While you're in the area of keeping your work space more enjoyable, take a few moments to neaten up. Give your desk a wipe-down and put away or shred unnecessary paperwork. Getting rid of clutter and having a neater work area puts you in a more positive frame of mind so you can take on the day.

DO SOME DESKSIDE YOGA

Take a quick stress break with a couple of yoga moves that help you stretch out while boosting energy, like these exercises from New York-based yoga instructor Kristin McGee.

Cleansing Breath Sit tall on chair, right hand on belly and left hand at side. Inhale deeply, then exhale all the way out. Next, take a partial breath in, then make small, sharp exhalations; aim for 80 to 100 pumping breaths.

High Altar Leans Sit tall, your feet hip-width apart on floor, hips toward the edge of the chair and back straight. Stretch arms in front of you, interlacing fingers with palms facing away from torso. Lift arms up and above head, keeping shoulders pressed down and elbows in line with ears. Then lean to the left as far as you can, keeping right hip on chair. Stay here for 5 breaths; come back to center and repeat on right. Do 2 to 3 times per side.

> **"HAVE AN ESTABLISHED PATTERN OF THINGS YOU TYPICALLY DO TO GET YOURSELF READY FOR THE WEEK AHEAD. "**
> —PSYCHOLOGIST MARGARET GREENBERG

LOVE THE WORK YOU DO

MOST OF US DEVOTE ABOUT A THIRD OF OUR DAYS TO OUR JOB. HERE'S HOW TO FIND MEANING IN YOUR CAREER

CULTIVATE BLISS

→ **HOW HAPPY ARE YOU** at work? Sure, we all have days when we dread our jobs, but for the most part, are you generally satisfied? According to Gallup's 2017 "State of the American Workplace" report, more than half of us (51 percent) are not engaged in what we do, and only about a third are satisfied with our employment.

That's a missed opportunity, since so much of who we are is defined by what we do. "When work is not a positive place, it can impact other pieces of your life in a negative way," notes positive psychologist Margaret Greenberg. To get more out of your working life and feel more satisfied about your job, try the following expert-approved strategies.

1
LOOK AT THE BIG PICTURE

Yale researcher Amy Wrzesniewski, Ph.D., has written about how most of us view our employment. Some people consider their job to be just that—a paycheck that's a means to an end, helping to support their families or hobbies, and they don't feel much connection to it. Others consider their work to be a career, something that's part of an upwardly mobile chain from which they can grow and learn. And still others feel their work is a calling, something they were simply meant to do. It's this last group that finds the most meaning and satisfaction from work and their lives.

2
KNOW YOUR STRENGTHS

Not sure if you're really in love with your job? Answer these three questions, says Greenberg: When am I at my best? What work really energizes me? What comes easily to me? "When we know what we do best and we use those skills every day, that's when our level of engagement and satisfaction goes up," she says.

3
FOCUS ON THE POSITIVE

"Happiness in the workplace can come in one of two ways: You can either do work that you already enjoy, or you can learn to enjoy what you are already doing," says Victor Shamas, Ph.D., a retired professor of psychology at the University of Arizona and author of *Deep Creativity*. Enjoying more of what you do can largely be a shift of perspective, he adds. "Sometimes jobs are just tasks that have to be done, but you can find satisfaction out of what you do by thinking about the positive impact you may have on others."

Looking for a career change? Take time to formulate a strategy before you jump ship, and don't be in a rush to find something new.

4

ENRICH YOUR SITUATION

Sometimes all it takes to feel better on the job is to make your workplace a more enjoyable one. Hang up some photos of loved ones or photos of beautiful scenery. If you're able, put on some music that makes you feel good. "It's the old whistle-while-you-work idea," says Shamas. "A positive attitude can make all the difference to your satisfaction."

5

BE HONEST WITH YOURSELF

"Your job has to be in line with your core values. When those are violated, that's when your sense of engagement or happiness goes down," notes Christine Mann, an executive coach and head of Mann Consulting in Scottsdale, Arizona. "Consider what really makes you happy, and then decide if you are willing to make the sacrifices it may take to facilitate that change."

6

TRY AN EXPERIMENT

"If we're bored or dissatisfied, that could be a good sign it's time to do something different," Greenberg says. But you don't have to give your notice tomorrow. Put some feelers out first: Take a class in an area you're interested in, volunteer with a group you want to spend more time with or interview others in the field you want to pursue.

7

FORM A PLAN

If you decide it's time for a job or career change, map out what that will look like. "You need a strategic plan before you cut any cords," Mann advises. Make a vision statement, then plan your strategy for the next three to six months. Keep checking in with yourself to make sure you're on track.

8

TAKE A CHANCE

"Most people tend to regret errors of omission," says Shamas. "They regret the things they didn't do more than the ones they did." If you're not ready to make a leap, try floating a trial balloon. Send out a résumé, or start a small business on the side with just a few customers. "You never know what that will turn into, and you'll also never know if you don't try."

9

REMEMBER, IT'S NEVER TOO LATE

Not all of us want to head into retirement playing golf or spending time at home. "Often people decide they want to have an encore career—something that's meaningful and brings them a sense of purpose," says Greenberg. This might be the perfect time to finally do what you really enjoy, whether that's writing a book, teaching a class or starting your own business.

7.99
AVERAGE NUMBER OF HOURS WORKED ON A WEEKDAY

SOURCE U.S. DEPARTMENT OF LABOR BUREAU OF LABOR STATISTICS

Ready to move on? Create a vision plan with specific steps.

7 KEY SIGNS OF A HAPPY WORKER

PART OF THE 2017 WORLD HAPPINESS REPORT EXPLORED WHAT MAKES EMPLOYEES HAPPY AROUND THE GLOBE. IT USED DATA FROM THE GALLUP WORLD POLL, WHICH COVERS MORE THAN 150 COUNTRIES WORLDWIDE, REPRESENTING 98 PERCENT OF THE WORLD'S POPULATION. HERE'S A LOOK AT WHAT WORKERS REPORTED BROUGHT THEM THE MOST SATISFACTION WITH THEIR JOBS:

1 **Good pay**
2 **Work-life balance**
3 **Job variety**
4 **Learning new information or skills**
5 **Individual autonomy**
6 **Job security**
7 **Coworker support**

HAVE A HAPPIER COMMUTE

GETTING TO AND FROM OUR JOB IS ONE OF THE BIGGEST STRESSORS MANY OF US FACE EACH DAY. AND THE LONGER OUR COMMUTE, THE GREATER OUR ANXIETY. RATHER THAN GETTING EMOTIONALLY CAUGHT UP IN TRAFFIC OR AN OVERLY CROWDED BUS, "CREATE RITUALS FOR YOURSELF," SAYS STANFORD RESEARCHER LEAH WEISS, PH.D. "PLAN YOUR TIME INTENTIONALLY, AND KEEP YOUR ATTENTION WHERE YOU ARE."

IF YOU DRIVE Start off enjoying five minutes of silence. "It's an experience we don't have during the day," Weiss says. "Use it as a time to be where you are and see what you are feeling physically and emotionally." Then tune into a podcast that teaches you something you want to learn about. "Curiosity is such an important thing, and learning and having a growth mindset is something we cultivate through mindfulness, so this is similar in nature," she explains.

IF YOU TAKE PUBLIC TRANSIT Practice compassion with the people in the bus or subway car around you. "Focus on the humanity of the moment. Everyone around you is someone who matters," Weiss says. If you find yourself judging, remind yourself, 'I have no idea what he has been through, but he's human, so he's probably been through some hard times.' This helps you become more aware of your reactions.

IF YOU BIKE OR WALK Really home in on the physical sensations of where you are going (while still paying attention to traffic and your surroundings, of course!). How do your feet feel when they hit the ground? Or the wind feel against your face as you move? "We can use our commute as 'zone out' time, but this is using it as 'pay attention' time and savoring what you are doing to train your awareness," Weiss says.

ANYTIME YOU'RE CAUGHT IN TRAFFIC Take a deep breath. Breathe in as fully as possible, hold that breath for a few moments, then exhale as fully as possible. Do this again. And again. "This time-tested and science-validated approach doesn't just make us feel better mentally, it relieves physical tension," Weiss says. The more you breathe, the more relaxed you'll be and the better you'll feel—even when you're staring at the taillights stuck in front of you.

CLEAN SLATE

DECLUTTERING YOUR HOME CAN DO A LOT TO NEATEN UP YOUR HEADSPACE AS WELL AS YOUR LIVING AREA

CULTIVATE BLISS

→ **WHEN I SIT DOWN** to work in my home office, the pile of stacked paperwork doesn't exactly spark my creativity. And thanks to my status as a clotheshorse who owns a tiny closet, just opening my bedroom door leads to a similar feeling of being a bit overwhelmed by all that stuff.

I'm not alone. Most of us, at one point, have had that sense of just needing to purge some of our goods that have piled up over the years, and the liberating feeling that comes with having a clean space.

Best-selling author Marie Kondo neatly captured this sentiment through her book *The Life-Changing Magic of Tidying Up: The Japanese Art of Decluttering and Organizing*. The guide has flown off shelves since it was first published in 2014, selling more than 4 million copies around the world as people took her advice to heart while paring down their homes.

CLEAR SPACE, CLEAR HEAD

But for Kondo, cleaning up isn't just about having a neater space—the mental state that accompanies it is just as important. She's seen clients' lives transformed after they tidy up according to her methods. "When you put your house in order, you put your affairs and your past in order too," she writes in *The Life-Changing Magic of Tidying Up*. "In essence, tidying ought to be the act of restoring balance among people, their possessions and the house they live in…. It's a very strange phenomenon, but when we reduce what we own and essentially 'detox' our house, it has a detoxifying effect on our bodies as well."

After being tired of looking at a mound of papers on my desk all day and not being able to fit one more single thing in my closet, I decided to give my own place the Kondo treatment, hoping I could clear up some space, too, both physically and mentally.

Kondo's tactics are all about paring down, even if you have to be ruthless about it. As a New York City resident, my space is too small and I have too much stuff, so I delved into her purge methods. Kondo's way is to tackle things by category—not room or location—since she says all like items should be stored together. She believes the best sequence is starting with clothes, then books, papers, miscellaneous items and ending with mementos.

KEEP OR TOSS?

Kondo advises taking every single item and putting it in a pile on the floor to ensure that you thoroughly examine each one. Her philosophy is that if something doesn't "spark joy" when you touch it, then it's time to toss it. While I'm not completely on board with that reasoning (my down coat doesn't spark joy, but I certainly need it for frigid northeastern winters), I applied it to a few things in my closet that I felt pretty "meh" about. Rounding up a couple of bags of clothes to donate did feel pretty cathartic.

Paperwork proves another challenge for me, since as a full-time freelance writer, I often work from home and have the files to prove it. "I recommend you dispose of anything that does not fall into one of three categories: currently in use, needed for a limited period of time or must be kept indefinitely," Kondo writes. At her recommendation, I toss all instruction manuals, since those are all online now, and old unnecessary pay stubs.

"WHEN WE REDUCE WHAT WE OWN, AND ESSENTIALLY DETOX OUR HOUSE, IT HAS A DETOXIFYING EFFECT ON OUR BODIES."
—MARIE KONDO, AUTHOR, *THE LIFE-CHANGING MAGIC OF TIDYING UP*

Clean out your closets over several days instead of a few stressful hours.

HOLDING ON

"By handling each sentimental item and deciding what to discard, you process your past," Kondo writes. "When we really delve into the reasons for why we can't let something go, there are only two: an attachment to the past or a fear for the future." I'm certainly guilty of hanging on to sentimental items. "Presents are not 'things' but a means for conveying someone's feelings," Kondo writes. A few more things make the donation pile.

After discarding, the second action of Kondo's method is deciding where to store items. "Clutter is caused by a failure to return things to where they belong. Therefore, storage should reduce the effort needed to put things away, not the effort to get them out," Kondo writes. She's not a fan of storage containers—a plain old shoebox is her go-to—so I try to find a simple home for everything instead. "The point in deciding specific places to keep things is to designate a spot for every thing," Kondo writes. While I have already heeded her advice about folding everything that can be folded, I make sure that all my items have a specific home, since Kondo states that not having to search for anything is a major stress reliever.

After the work is done, I feel relieved when I open my closet door to see a pared-down space. Even sitting at a more minimal (and newly neatened up) desk eases some stress. As Kondo writes, "The question of what you own is actually the question of how you want to live your life."
—*Celia Shatzman*

GETTING RID OF CLUTTER ELIMINATES 40 PERCENT OF HOUSEWORK IN AN AVERAGE-SIZE HOME.

EASY LIVING

A FEW SIMPLE DECORATING STRATEGIES CAN MAKE YOU FEEL MORE MINDFUL AT HOME

Marie Kondo isn't the only organizer who believes that a clean home equals a clear mind. "When we have a mess in our outside space, it often stems from a mess inside our headspace," says Amelia Meena, owner of Appleshine, a professional lifestyle organizing company. "We believe you should surround yourself with things that are creative, inspiring, positive and empowering."

Decluttering your home helps you refine your priorities. "You can unclog the things that slow you down, cost you more money and waste your time. When you move out items that you no longer need, your efficiency increases. You're no longer wasting money on things you already own but can't find," Meena adds. Ready to create a more mindful living space? Start by following these simple tactics.

GO GREEN What element speaks to you the most? If the beach calls your name, hang up an inspiring image of the ocean. More of an earthy type? Bring in plants—even fake ones—to brighten the space with greenery. Added bonus: Research shows plants can help fight indoor pollution.

THROW IT OUT Toss (or recycle) junk mail before you even get through your front door. You'll reduce the piles of clutter that tend to accumulate.

FIND INSPIRATION Surround yourself with items that inspire you, whether it's an image from a favorite artist or a photo from your last vacation. Just be careful not to overdo it, since that can create a mental distraction. A wall of books may be nice but can consume precious space. Instead, keep just a few of your favorite books stacked on your desk or bedside table, where you'll see them often.

MAKE A DATE Schedule a time to edit, purge and donate at least three to four times a year. Mark your calendar for the end of every season to stay on track.

CHOOSE A HUE Pick a color scheme to carry throughout the surrounding space. Too many competing colors and variety of materials create visual chaos.

EMBRACE YOUR SPACE Make an effort to define a large, empty space. In a closet, consider a redesign that allows for shelves or additional hanging space rather than just one rod and one shelf. In a drawer, use dividers to create different categories.

THINK THINGS THROUGH Pay attention to your actions and habits. If you're always tossing your clothes on the floor, get a hamper to contain them. If you drop your keys on the kitchen table, find a dish to hold them. While some habits may need tweaking, others just need acknowledgment so they can work for you, not against you.

ADD WISELY Be mindful of what you bring into your home. In addition to being conscious of what you purchase, also consider politely declining free or re-gifted items. Simply say, "No, thank you."

A CALL TO
ACTION

ALWAYS PUTTING THINGS OFF? HERE'S
HOW TO STOP PROCRASTINATING SO YOU CAN
FEEL BETTER ABOUT EVERYTHING YOU DO

TO DO LIST

1. CLEAN GARAGE
2. WASH THE DOG
3. TAKE OUT TRASH
4. PICK UP KIDS
5. DROP OFF KIDS
6. PAY BABYSITTER
7. GROCERY SHOP
8. MEET TEACHERS
9. BAKE MUFFINS
10. PICK UP SHIRTS
11. MEET w/ PTA!
12. START NEW LIST

Make a list of your tasks—then check them off when each one is done.

→ **THERE'S A PARTICULAR DRAWER** in my kitchen that seems to attract clutter. You may know the type. It's a catchall for everything from safety pins to sticky notes, matches to markers, and an ever-growing pile of takeout menus, receipts, stamps, pens and much more. Every few months, I get inspired to dump everything out in an attempt to instill order amid the chaos. And despite the fact that there are much bigger sections of my home that I need to purge (closets, cabinets, you name it), spending just a half hour or so on this one small corner of my kitchen leaves me with no small sense of accomplishment —and a measure of happiness that lasts far longer than it took me to get the job done.

Licensed clinical psychologist Rachel Hershenberg, Ph.D., an assistant professor of psychiatry and behavioral sciences at Emory University in Atlanta and the author of *Activating Happiness: A Jump-Start Guide to Overcoming Low Motivation, Depression, or Just Feeling Stuck,* explains why cleaning out the junk drawer—or tackling a similarly small task head-on—can make you feel better. "We all feel a sense of accomplishment from checking something off a to-do list," says Hershenberg. "There's a certain satisfaction you get from finishing a task or reaching a goal that gives you extra energy to go ahead and do something else."

So it makes sense that the opposite action— putting off a challenge or simply procrastinating on a chore, a job or an obligation—can have a negative effect on our psyche. It may not happen the first time, or even the 10th. But avoiding these micro-acts or activities can create a downward spiral of negative thoughts, emotions and behaviors, Hershenberg explains.

PROCRASTINATION NATION

We all procrastinate from time to time. In fact, in this day and age, who among us hasn't gone down a rabbit hole of social media posts and article links that take us far from the original task. (I recently spent 45 minutes with the intention of checking the weather and found myself engrossed swiping through images of adorable dogs catching treats off their snouts.)

"Procrastination is a universal issue. It's so common to get distracted: You log on to your computer to pay a bill and then get sidetracked by an e-mail that comes in that leads you to search a term and takes you to another Web page," says Hershenberg. "Before you know it, half the evening has gone by."

Procrastinating can also spill over into other areas of our lives. Maybe you're up way past your usual bedtime, watching an episode of your favorite show on Netflix, and just as the closing credits come on, you start to feel a sense of dread. You don't want the show to end, because that means you have to go to sleep and head to work the next day. "You may start to feel anxious just from this simple action of the show ending," says Hershenberg. You may even feel a physical response, like your heart rate increasing and your breathing

"THERE'S A SATISFACTION YOU GET FROM FINISHING A TASK THAT GIVES YOU EXTRA ENERGY."
—PSYCHOLOGIST RACHEL HERSHENBERG

becoming more shallow. The easiest thing to do? Queue up the next episode and sit back and continue to watch, even if that means you'll be tired and cranky the next day because you haven't gotten enough sleep.

TAKING ACTION

But by taking some simple steps to overcome this act of procrastination, notes Hershenberg, you can help cut off the downward spiral and regain a measure of control—and happiness. She advises her clients to follow a "T.R.A.P." —Trigger, emotional Response and Action Pattern— technique and notes the consequences these actions may bring.

Take the case of the Netflix night. Here, says Hershenberg, the trigger is the end of the show, followed by your emotional response (those feelings of dread and having the urge to put things off and keep watching). Next comes the action pattern: "Do you follow the urge to avoid going to sleep by continuing to watch your show, even though it will make you more tired the next day, or do you shut it off and go to sleep?" asks Hershenberg.

Recognizing your triggers, emotional responses and action patterns, then employing specific coping strategies can help you overcome chronic procrastination, so you learn to do more and put things off less. "We can be very hard on ourselves when we put things off.

Ultimately, however, that can deplete your resources," she notes.

In this case, she says, you might want to find something you can do to ease yourself into sleep, whether that's putting on a playlist or talking to your bed partner. "See if you can find a strategy that's not going to still have you up 45 minutes later," Hershenberg says. Then monitor your behavior to see if your new strategy works.

Incorporating some deep-breathing techniques after you identify the trigger can also help. "If you start by changing what is going on in your body, you can have an influence over your emotions," Hershenberg explains. For example, if you feel yourself getting nervous about putting off a task, taking some deep, calming breaths will help your body start to feel calmer, too. It can be as simple as taking 30 to 60 seconds to catch your breath and think about what you will do next. "That will ultimately influence your decision-making process," says the professor.

You can also apply the "T.R.A.P." technique to other areas of your life as a way to identify and understand patterns of procrastination, says Hershenberg. "Maybe you always procrastinate at a certain time of day, or you'll habitually check e-mails instead of following your to-do list."

Monitoring these habits can help you identify them so you can halt the procrastination cycle, she adds. And the more you move forward, the better (and ultimately happier) you will feel.

SIMPLE STEPS TO OVERCOME DRAGGING YOUR FEET CAN HELP YOU REGAIN CONTROL.

Identify where you tend to put things off in your life—then make an action plan to get past those roadblocks.

PART 4

EASY WAYS TO FIND YOUR JOY

DISCOVERING SIMPLE PLEASURES ALL AROUND YOU

FINDING JOY

21
SUPER-QUICK HAPPINESS HACKS

START SMILING ASAP WITH THESE SIMPLE PICK-ME-UPS!

→ **EVER HAVE THAT DAY** when every little thing seems to go wrong and you want to jump back into bed and get a fresh start tomorrow? Don't crawl under the covers just yet: These research-backed tips can help you banish your funky mood and feel cheerful, energized and happier in less time than it takes to finish a cappuccino.

1

START PLANNING YOUR NEXT VACATION

Sure it's fun to get away, but research shows that looking forward to a trip often brings more joy than the vacation itself. In a study of 1,550 participants, vacationers reported a higher degree of pre-trip happiness compared to those who didn't travel— but only those who took a very relaxed trip felt happier once they were back home.

2

JOT DOWN WHAT YOU'RE GRATEFUL FOR

Keeping track of the things you appreciate can improve your mood and your health. Researchers have found that practicing gratitude can boost your immunity, help you sleep better, reduce depression symptoms and even increase the amount of time you exercise by an average of one and a half hours a week compared to people who focused on the negatives in their lives. And even on the crummiest of days, reflecting on a few small pleasures can change your mindset to a positive one. To reap the positive effects of gratitude, consider writing in a journal. You might want to jot down some of the good things that happened to you or find some positives you can be grateful for, whether that's a warm bed, a hot shower or your kids' health. Then you'll always have somewhere to turn to when you need a pick-me-up.

3

PICK UP A LITERARY NOVEL

Reading Jane Austen or Charles Dickens may help you have a better understanding of other people's emotions, a skill that's important to our social relationships, according to research. Joining a book club may also boost happiness. A University of Liverpool study of subjects suffering from depression found that when they read literature and engaged in discussions, they enhanced their psychological well-being.

4

VISIT YOUR NEAREST BEACH

If you're lucky enough to live near a shoreline, put your toes in the sand. Research shows spending time gazing at the ocean and breathing in sea air is good for your mental health. An English census data report found that people who lived near the coast reported better physical and mental health than those who didn't, and a study published in the *Journal of Coastal Zone Management* said that participants who have ocean views report feeling calmer than those without it. Can't get away? Check out websites with sea views and sounds like Calm.com or watch a YouTube video of crashing waves in a tropical setting.

5

SNIFF AN UPLIFTING SCENT

Deeply inhaling certain odors can make you feel happier. Among the top scent boosters: citrus, peppermint, eucalyptus and rosemary. Consider keeping small vials of these essential oils in your desk drawer at work to sniff when energy lags. Even better, eat an orange or sip peppermint tea in the afternoon.

6

DONATE TO A CHARITY

If you want to change your attitude for the better, do something nice for someone else. "Giving," whether that's of your time or money, activates the areas of the brain that also light up during pleasurable activities like sex and eating certain foods. There is also a causal relationship between people who tend to donate money and life satisfaction. Find a charity that strikes a chord with your values and give what you can. Have more free time? Volunteer in your community: Research shows it can boost happiness by increasing life satisfaction and providing a sense of purpose.

7

NIBBLE DARK CHOCOLATE

Numerous studies have confirmed what most of us already instinctively know—eating chocolate makes you happy. And research published in the journal *Nutrients* found dark chocolate can help boost concentration and memory. Scientists speculate that both the flavonols and plant compounds found in cacao play a role in chocolate's mood-enhancing effects.

8

GO ON A WALK

Almost any kind of exercise can make you feel happier and give you a sense of accomplishment. And it doesn't take hours of action to reap the benefits. Research shows that doing just five minutes a day of any outdoor activity (walking, cycling, running) can almost immediately improve mood.

9

DO A GOOD DEED

Whether you offer to take out the trash for your spouse or donate to a charity, performing an act of kindness benefits you as well as the recipient. As Mark Twain wrote, "The best way to cheer yourself is to try to cheer somebody else up." And science seconds his teachings: One study found that doing kind acts for others can improve overall life satisfaction in as little as 10 days.

10

EAT PROTEIN-RICH FOODS

Foods like meat, poultry, nuts and milk often contain the essential amino acid tryptophan, which helps form the production of the brain chemical serotonin. Numerous studies show that low levels of serotonin can contribute to a lowered mood state. (And no, the tryptophan in your Thanksgiving turkey isn't what makes you sleepy—you can blame that on how much food you pile on your plate.) So go ahead and enjoy that sizzling steak!

11

HAVE A TALL GLASS OF H_2O

If you're feeling lethargic and a bit cranky to boot, there's a good chance you're dehydrated. That can be true even if you've chugged a venti latte for an energy boost this morning—caffeine can act as a mild diuretic, so your body might not be as hydrated as you think. Make sure you drink water in the morning before your coffee, then sip a few more glasses throughout the day. Just how much water you need varies by person, according to the Mayo Clinic. But an "adequate" intake is defined as 15.5 cups of all types of fluids daily for men and 11.5 cups daily for women. Aim to hit or surpass that mark, and try to make as much of your fluid intake as possible plain old H_2O.

12

TURN ON A FAVORITE SONG

If you're stuck in traffic or need a boost to get through the final stages of a project, turn up the volume. Listening to songs that make you feel energized can send a bad mood packing, according to research involving music therapy and depression. So whether your jam is "Uptown Funk," "Take Me to Church" or another tune that makes you feel good, have your music on hand for whenever you need to smile.

13

TAKE A HOT BATH

Or find some other healthy distraction. After all, when we feel stressed or anxious, it's all too easy to turn to unhealthy methods to cope—hello, big bottle of Chablis! But when you're really bogged down with negative feelings, try finding a beneficial distraction to lift your mood, suggests positive psychologist Barbara Fredrickson, Ph.D., in her book *Positivity*. Make a list of healthy distractions you can turn to the next time you feel down and out. Think: Go for a jog, take a warm bath, do some yoga, fix your bike or sit down with a steamy cup of tea. Anything that helps you feel good and puts your worries to the side for a bit can help.

14

WAKE UP EARLY, OPEN THE SHADES

Exposing yourself to natural light helps your body stop producing melatonin—the hormone that makes you sleepy—and promotes wakefulness. Take a walk outside to let the sun's UVB rays hit your skin so your body produces vitamin D.

15

STOP COMPLAINING

When you become aware of your complaints, you're better able to detach yourself from negative thoughts and find a more neutral reaction, says Elisha Goldstein, Ph.D., author of *Uncovering Happiness*. Next time you have a negative thought, be attuned to how it affects you. Being aware can help you fight the knee-jerk urge to complain.

16

PLAY WITH A POOCH

Therapy dogs have long been used to help decrease stress and lessen symptoms of anxiety and depression in people who suffer from post-traumatic stress disorder (PTSD) or who live in nursing homes. But research shows spending even just a few minutes with animals can also help the rest of us reduce our levels of tension and stress.

FINDING JOY

17

ACKNOWLEDGE SOMEONE ELSE'S JOY
Seeing people who are loving life can help boost
your own mood, says Goldstein, cofounder of New
York City's Center for Mindful Living. When you spy
people laughing or enjoying themselves, instead
of thinking "Why am I not happy?" turn it around
and see if you can summon up an encouraging
thought about their good moment. For example:
"I'm happy you're happy." This helps you conjure up
what researchers call "relational positivity"—your
pleasure neurons in your brain will start to fire and
you can literally catch some of their good vibes.

18

TURN OFF NEGATIVE NEWS
Constantly hearing about shootings, wars and
other violent events on the news can be a major
bummer. Of course, staying informed is important,
but you may be able to reduce some of the
gratuitous negative news. Fredrickson suggests
asking: "How can I alter my media diet to cut some
of that out?" You may find there's more good news
out there than you realized.

19

DOWNLOAD A GAME

Science says that trying something new or honing a new skill stimulates and challenges your brain, particularly if what you're doing puts you in a state of "flow"—when you lose track of time because you're in a mental state of complete absorption. Take a five-minute break from work to research a new recipe to try, play a new game on your smartphone, fill out a crossword puzzle or play free brain games online.

20

REMEMBER A HAPPY MOMENT

Our brain has an unfortunate tendency to focus on what's going wrong. From an evolutionary standpoint, this pessimistic mindset used to help us stay aware of dangers, says Goldstein. But today, those negative thoughts often get too much attention. When things feel glum, refer back to a time when you felt happy. Goldstein calls these "joy breaks." And try to bask in these moments when they first occur. Think: "This is a good moment. Can I allow myself to linger in it?" he suggests. "If we want to be happier, we have to look out for our own good moments and deepen them."

21

FIND SOME FLOWERS

Pick up a pretty bouquet to set on your kitchen table or bring an arrangement for your desk at work. A study from Harvard University found that people reported being happier and more energetic after looking at flowers first thing in the morning, especially if the buds were displayed in a room where they spent a lot of time.

FEEL-GOOD MOVES

FOR A QUICK, EFFECTIVE AND LONG-LASTING MOOD BOOST, IT PAYS TO BE PHYSICALLY ACTIVE

→ **WHETHER YOU'VE HAD A FIGHT** with a friend, a tough day at work or just need a pick-me-up, there's one guaranteed way to feel better: get moving. A huge amount of research cements the link between physical activity and mental health, from alleviating depression and reducing anxiety to putting more pep in your step.

But it's not just about lacing up your shoes. "We used to think all exercise would make people feel better, but now we know that's too general of a conclusion," explains Panteleimon Ekkekakis, Ph.D., a professor in the department of kinesiology at Iowa State University. "Exercise has enormous potential for both short- and long-term mental health benefits, but there are certain conditions attached." To get the most out of your workouts, consider the following guidelines.

FINDING JOY

Whether you
run, walk, bike
or hike, just a
few minutes of
exercise can help
you feel happier.

WORK HARD (BUT NOT TOO HARD) The best way to boost your mood is to raise your heart rate, Ekkekakis says. "The most prominent effects on mood are seen at a moderate intensity level," he notes. Since intensity is highly individual (one person's jog can be another's all-out sprint), an easy way to determine the appropriate level is the "Talk Test"—how difficult it is to maintain a conversation during exercise. At a moderate intensity, you should be a little breathless. If you're able to say long sentences without huffing and puffing, you might want to take things up a notch. But if you can only get a couple of words out at a time, it's a good idea to dial things down, since a very high intensity can be uncomfortable.

DON'T GIVE UP Exercise can be unpleasant if you're not used to it. And researchers say having some fitness base is important when it comes to boosting your mood. "Exercise can be challenging for overweight and obese people, so it might not make them feel better," says Ekkekakis. "There's often some aches and pains involved." That ultimately all goes away—but you have to stick with it.

CHOOSE YOUR FAVORITE It doesn't really matter what form of physical activity you do: Whether you're running, walking, swimming, cycling, doing yoga or dancing up a storm, any form of exercise that gets you moving can have a positive effect on your mood. The exercise doesn't even have to be aerobic. Research shows that older adults with depression experienced significant reduction in symptoms after 10 weeks of strength training (while also improving strength, morale and quality of life). And a 2014 study found that both yoga and strength training helped reduce symptoms of depression. "There's a powerful sense of achievement that accompanies many forms of exercise—a sense that you're able to complete something that wasn't necessarily easy to do," says Ekkekakis. "All of that plays into how you feel."

BLOW OFF STEAM "Almost everyone derives some kind of benefit from exercise if they are experiencing some level of stress or anxiety," notes John Bartholomew, Ph.D., professor and chair in the department of Kinesiology and Health Education at the University of Texas at Austin. Boss yell at you in a meeting? Did you get into a spat with your spouse? Stand up and take a walk. It won't solve all of your problems, but you'll feel better in the short term.

GO OUTSIDE Although movement itself can make you feel better, getting some fresh air while you're doing it seems to increase the effect. "Being outside in a natural setting can help improve your mood even if you aren't exercising, but being physically active can provide added benefits," says Ekkekakis. One recent Austrian study found subjects who hiked in the mountains had higher mood scores and felt the exercise was less strenuous than when they completed a similar-intensity workout on a treadmill.

MAKE IT MINDFUL You may already know about the benefits of mindfulness when it comes to mood. But you can also incorporate mindfulness into your workout, says William Pullen, a London-based therapist and the author of *Running with Mindfulness: Dynamic Running Therapy to Improve Low-Mood, Anxiety, Stress, and Depression.* He uses

FINDING JOY

Strength training has been shown to relieve symptoms of depression.

movement-based therapy with his clients to help them open up about their feelings. But you can also use it to help you become more in tune with your own emotions, he says.

Start by finding a comfortable pace and take a moment or two to become aware of your surroundings—the colors, the shapes, the smells, the weather. Remind yourself of your intention to run (or walk) mindfully. Choose a foot and count each time it hits the ground. Count 10 steps, then start again at number one and continue for a while. If other thoughts come, acknowledge them and return to counting your steps. If the thoughts continue, keep returning to your counting. If your body is in pain, slow down or stop, but try to get to the point where you are in a zone, experiencing each step as it comes.

DON'T BE TOO HARD ON YOURSELF If you thrive on competition, then races and games may seem ideal—but try not to get yourself too crazy. "Some athletes can be very hypercritical and can suffer from depression," says Bartholomew. "Try not to get to the point of judging yourself too harshly based on the outcome of your activity."

KEEP IT UP Exercise is good for your mood but also for your mind, helping to slow or minimize some of the mental changes that can come with aging, such as memory loss and dementia. "There's no known drug out there that has been able to reliably restore cognitive deficits associated with aging, but exercise has been shown to halt or at least slow the decline," says Ekkekakis. Some research shows memory recall can even improve after exercise. And it doesn't take a lot: "Even just one to two hours a week of moderate-intensity activity like walking can help bring about these improvements," he adds.

4 WAYS
EXERCISE MAKES YOU FEEL BETTER

EVER WONDER WHY EVERYTHING SEEMS
A LITTLE BIT ROSIER AFTER YOU'VE WORKED
UP A SWEAT? HERE'S WHAT SCIENTISTS
THINK IS HAPPENING INSIDE YOUR HEAD

1

Endorphins Are Released We've all heard about the feel-good brain chemicals called endorphins that seem to be behind the "runner's high" phenomenon. But endorphins only really kick in at higher intensity levels. "Endorphins start to be produced when the body is challenged as a way to conquer some of the stress you are feeling," says Panteleimon Ekkekakis, Ph.D. "This generally won't happen when you're exercising at a moderate or low intensity."

2

Serotonin Is Produced One reason that exercise may be so effective in fighting depression is the amount of mood-boosting serotonin it produces. When you exercise, your brain is bathed in serotonin, acting much like antidepressant medications that prevent the reabsorption of serotonin in the brain. In fact, research has shown that exercise is just as effective as antidepressant drugs for patients with major depressive disorder.

3

You Get a Little High Your brain produces another class of chemicals, called endocannabinoids, that are chemically similar to the drug cannabis. "These neurotransmitters are associated with the same type of pleasure you get when you eat an appetizing meal or engage in sexual activity," Ekkekakis notes. Luckily, it only takes a moderate level of activity for your brain to start to produce these chemical messengers.

4

Your Brain Gets a Bit Bigger Depression can shrink the hippocampus, the part of the brain that deals with memory. Certain antidepression drugs try to stop this reduction by increasing the proteins (neurotrophins) that help create new neurons. Exercise can also increase neurotrophins and may be even more effective than the drugs at preventing a loss of brain matter. "Exercise can restore the size of the hippocampus in people with depression without the side effects of medication," Ekkekakis says.

HUGGING
IT OUT

HOW PHYSICAL TOUCH CAN BENEFIT
YOUR WHOLE BODY—NO ROMANCE REQUIRED

→ **WHEN WAS THE LAST TIME** you received a good hug—not just a quick clutch, but the kind where it feels like the person really cares about you and is sending you love and goodwill? A great embrace not only makes you feel calmer and reassured, it has physical and psychological effects as well.

"Touch is not only nice, it's needed," says Kathleen Keating Schloessinger, R.N., author of *The Hug Therapy Book.* "Scientific research supports the theory that stimulation by touch is absolutely necessary for our physical as well as our emotional well-being."

Why does touch help us heal? The skin's sensory nerve endings are hooked up to the part of the brain that handles emotional responses. When you're touched in a pleasurable way (not just in a sexual one), your brain gets the message that you're feeling safe and secure, says Schloessinger.

But physical touch has a variety of other benefits for both our body and brain. For one, hugs have been shown to help lower levels of the stress hormone cortisol. That's true even if the "hug" comes from a huggable human-shaped device rather than a person, according to a study published in the journal *Nature.* Reduced cortisol can also help boost your immune response and protect your body against illness and infection. In a 2015 study from Carnegie Mellon University, participants who perceived they had greater social support (as measured in part by receiving hugs) were only a third as likely to come down with a cold after being exposed to a virus. And those who did succumb to the sniffles reported less severe symptoms when they felt they had greater social support.

Brain studies have shown that hugs also increase levels of the "cuddle" hormone oxytocin, which helps reduce heart rate and lower stress hormones. A 2005 study from the University of North Carolina at Chapel Hill found women who reported more frequent hugs from their partners had higher measurable levels of oxytocin and lower resting blood pressure than those who were less frequently embraced. Touch and the tactile stimulation of stroking have even been shown to help reduce some of the pain intensity that women feel in the early stages of labor. MRI scans show areas in the brain lighting up during or after a hug.

Hugging also has measurable benefits that stretch beyond the physical. Research shows that receiving a hug, embrace or touch helps us feel less lonely, and that embraces can help reduce anxiety. And those who don't receive this type of positive physical contact—sometimes called "touch hungry"—are more likely to be depressed. Being touched has even allowed study participants to be better at decoding the other person's feelings of happiness and sadness compared to moments when they weren't experiencing the contact.

JANUARY 21

NATIONAL HUGGING DAY—IT HAS BEEN CELEBRATED WORLDWIDE SINCE 1986 AND INCLUDES EVENTS, PARTIES AND EVEN A "MOST HUGGABLE PEOPLE OF THE YEAR" AWARD. FOR MORE INFO, CHECK OUT NATIONALHUGGINGDAY.COM

We have an innate
ability to decode
emotions through
touch alone.

FINDING JOY

32%

AMOUNT BY WHICH REGULAR HUGS HELPED REDUCE THE LIKELIHOOD OF DEVELOPING A COLD AFTER BEING EXPOSED TO THE VIRUS

HOW TO HUG

YOU'VE PROBABLY BEEN GIVING HUGS SINCE THE TIME YOU WERE FIRST ABLE TO GRASP ON TO YOUR PARENT'S NECK. BUT THERE ARE A FEW THINGS TO KEEP IN MIND WHEN YOU'RE GIVING A MEANINGFUL EMBRACE

1

Have Intent

When you give somebody a hug, put some meaning into it, author Kathleen Keating Schloessinger says. "Make sure the hug shows that you really do care and that you're extending compassion and kindness," she adds.

2

Keep It Clean

Hugging someone in a nonromantic way should feel caring and comforting— which is very different from a lover's embrace, says Schloessinger. "Hugs should feel compassionate, not passionate," she notes. Center your feelings and thoughts around the original purpose of the hug, which is to offer mutual support and care.

3

Ask If It's OK

Be certain you have permission before giving a hug, Keating advises, and make sure you ask someone if you need one, too. Try: "May I give you a hug?" or "Could you use a hug?"

4

Make Contact

You don't always need to touch skin to skin to feel the healing benefits. In many studies, simply touching the shoulder, back or head brought about benefits. While touch is not as powerful as a full hug, it definitely has impact, says Schloessinger. If a friend is sharing something she's upset about, consider holding her hand or touching her arm to offer comfort.

5

Open Up

Be aware that receiving a hug or other close touch can open up emotions that were buried. "Touch can make people feel vulnerable," Schloessinger says. "You're softening yourself and you're softening the other person. When you soften and have pain, suffering, loss or something you haven't fully worked through, those emotions can come through."

EMBRACE A STRANGER?

Need a good hug? Consider joining a Cuddle Party. The group, now worldwide, was created to help others enjoy what it feels like to get close in a nonsexual way. "Cuddle Party is a great playground for discovering more about yourself, exploring new ways of connecting with others or simply enjoying a relaxing, cozy evening with other cuddly souls," says the company's website. Trained facilitators are on hand to help provide support and make sure all the cuddlers are playing by the rules. Tickets start at around $20. For more information, go to cuddleparty.com.

HEAD FIRST

DEVELOPING A SENSE OF MINDFULNESS CAN MINIMIZE DAILY STRESS AND PROVIDE LASTING HAPPINESS

→ CAN HAPPINESS REALLY STICK
around? Meeting friends for dinner, playing
with your kids or burying your toes in the
sand on a beach all sound like perfect ways to
feel joyful. But more often than not, these
moments tend to be fleeting. While we may feel
happy for a few minutes, we soon move on to
the next emotion.

But if we become more aware of our feelings
and connections, we can build upon this sense of
fulfillment so it becomes more of a constant in
our lives. The key, experts say, is to develop a
greater sense of mindfulness. "Spikes of
happiness may be momentary, but being mindful
of your emotions and your surroundings can help
you develop a flow that's more sustainable,"
explains Anne Yusim, a psychiatrist in New York
City and the author of *Fulfilled: How the Science
of Spirituality Can Help You Live a Happier,
More Meaningful Life.*

And when things start to get hairy, Yusim
adds, being mindful can offer a measure of
protection: "It can help shelter you when things
go awry. And the more you can tap into it, the
more powerful it can be."

FINDING JOY

Build a reserve of restful
memories to draw upon
at times of stress.

THE MINDFULNESS REVOLUTION

What, exactly, is mindfulness, anyway, and why should we care about it when it comes to our happiness? Simply put, mindfulness is the practice of focusing our awareness on our thoughts, emotions, and sensations. "This enables you to be aware of a thought, emotion or sensation without actually identifying with it," says Yusim.

One of the key ideas of mindfulness is that thoughts and sensations can pass us by without being rooted. "Thoughts are not facts," says Yusim. That shift in perception gives you freedom to experience different emotions, good and bad and helps you take more control over your emotions. "When you are attentive to whatever is going on inside you, you are in a far better position to make good decisions in your life," writes Yusim. And that can help you fight some of the inevitable stress we all face. In fact, numerous studies show that mindfulness leads to increased control over negative emotions and decreased rumination.

DON'T WORRY, BE HAPPY

That brings us to another fundamental belief—that mindfulness can make you a happier person. Although meditation is just one form of mindfulness, the practice of meditation—simply sitting and listening to your body and your breath—can help you tune in to your thoughts and feelings, without judgment.

"The practice of meditation is a tool for achieving happiness," notes Light Watkins, a meditation teacher based in Los Angeles and the author of *Bliss More: How to Succeed in Meditation Without Really Trying*. And while it's easier to be mindful when you are happy (and less so, when you are angry, stressed or tired), it comes back to how you feel at your baseline. "Our factory setting is happiness," Watkins says. "Children are just happy naturally, but we tend to be less so as we get older and have more stress in our lives." The act of meditation helps to manage stress, reducing stress hormones like cortisol so you can get back to that baseline setting of being in a good mood, Watkins explains.

In other words, when you take the time to simply observe your feelings of stress rather than just reacting to the situation, you're more likely to shut down that fight-or-flight mode that all too often accompanies a stressful situation. "You experience neurological changes that allow you to be much more focused, calm and connected," says Yusim.

The following anyone-can-do-it meditation exercises can help increase your sense of mindfulness and build your baseline level of happiness. Experiment to see which works best for you, then try to use at least one method daily.

METHOD ONE
TAKING IT EASY

Many of us are put off by the idea of meditation because it feels a little too out-there. But you don't have to be kneeling on a mat or sitting in a candlelit room to reap the benefits of meditation, says Watkins. "You shouldn't have to work hard or be uncomfortable to meditate," he notes. Watkins teaches the "E.A.S.Y." approach to meditation (short for Embrace, Accept, Surrender, Yield). Here's how it works.

1 Sit comfortably (like you're binge-watching your favorite show).
2 Use an easy-to-see timing device (ideally not an alarm clock).
3 Calculate your finish time (aim for 10 to 20 minutes).
4 Passively think the sound *ah-hum*.
5 Let yourself simultaneously get lost in your thoughts. ("Avoid thought-shaming," says Watkins.)
6 When you remember that you're meditating, passively begin thinking *ah-hum* again.
7 Peek freely and often at the time.
8 Once you're done, wait a minute or two before opening your eyes.
9 Come out slowly.

METHOD TWO
MINDFUL BREATHING

Focusing on your breathing can be a powerful entry point to a meditation session. Yusim also recommends following the cloud metaphor for allowing your thoughts to float away. Begin with just five minutes a day, Yusim suggests, gradually increasing to 20 minutes if you can.

1 Sit in a comfortable position, eyes closed.
2 Inhale for a count of two; hold your breath for a count of four, then exhale for a count of eight.
3 Repeat this cycle five times, then begin to breathe naturally, focusing on your breath without trying to control it.
4 When a thought enters your mind label it. For instance, if you have a thought about what you have to do later today, you will say to yourself in your mind "I'm having a thought about what I have to do later today." If you have a thought about what you will have for dinner tonight, label that thought accordingly. Don't judge any of the thoughts that come to you—simply label them.
5 Imagine a cloud floating by in front of you. As the cloud floats by, imagine physically taking your thought out of your mind and placing it on the cloud. Then watch your thought float away.
6 Return your attention to your normal breathing. Continue to breathe until the next thought enters your head. Label this thought and then place it on a cloud and watch it float away. Repeat this process for the next five minutes. Try to do this for five full minutes to allow yourself to experience mindfulness.

METHOD THREE
PRACTICING PRESENCE

"The way to be present with whatever you're doing is to learn to focus completely on doing that one thing," Yusim writes. Choose one thing today you would like to be wholly and completely present for—it could be absolutely anything in your day, from drinking your morning cup of coffee to folding laundry. Take the following steps.

1 As you begin to do this activity, pay attention to every aspect of it.
2 Take a moment to consciously collect all the information about your experience through your touch, your eyes, your ears, your smell, and perhaps though your taste.
   a. How does this experience feel?
   b. What does it look like?
   c. How does it smell? Sound? Taste?
   d. What emotions come up as you do it?
   e. What is going on in your body as you undertake this experience?

Meditation can be done while you're moving or still.

3 Now, become aware of what thoughts enter your mind. As you become aware of your thoughts, you'll notice them jump to other things.
4 Use your awareness to gently bring yourself back to your present task. Keep gently returning your awareness back to the present moment, time and again.

METHOD FOUR
LOVING-KINDNESS

"Whenever you practice mindfulness, it's important to emphasize self-kindness," says Tara Cousineau, Ph.D. Practice not only being aware of the present but also being nonjudgmental. This Loving-Kindness meditation from Cousineau's book, *The Kindness Connection*, is based on a Buddhist practice, and it can help to cultivate happiness for yourself and for others.

1 Sit quietly. Begin by sitting with a straight posture and relax into it so that the posture evokes a sense of grace, strength and dignity. Gently place your hands on your lap or, if you desire, over your heart. Tune in to your natural breathing for a few minutes.
3 Focus attention on your heart space and body. Place your attention around your heart, in the middle of your chest, perhaps repeating words such as "love," "peace" or "warmth." As you say this, envision someone or something you feel caring toward, such as a child, loved one, pet or comforting object. This ignites feelings of affection and love. Let these feelings radiate through your whole body, holding you in a warm embrace.
3 Focus on phrases that evoke tenderness for you. Feel the sense of caring, love and healing wash over you. Softly say to yourself any of the following phrases and explore how they resonate within you.

- *"May I be well."*
- *"May I be healthy."*
- *"May I be happy."*
- *"May I feel at peace."*
- *"May I feel safe."*
- *"May I be at ease."*
- *"May I feel loved and cared for."*

4 Expand your tenderness to thoughts of a loved one. Envision a loved one or someone who evokes affection or respect. Offer this person feelings of warmth and caring, and wish him or her well with words like the ones above, replacing "I" with "you." (i.e., "May you be well." "May you be healthy," and so on.)
5 Wish a stranger well. Extend your warm feelings to someone you do not know, someone you feel neutral about, like a fellow commuter on the subway, a person crossing the street, the checkout person at the supermarket. Repeat the words offered in the previous list. ("May you be well...")
6 Offer a circle of warmth. Repeat the words to wish him or her well. ("May you be well....")
7 Extend wishes of well-being to the entire world. Broaden the warm wishes to include your greater community, whether a church group or a city, and then include the world at large.
8 Return to your body, yourself and your life. When you are ready to return, repeat the phrases that wish yourself well. Close the practice by gently letting the feelings of loving-kindness ease, then paying attention to your breathing. Slowly open your eyes.

Mindfulness helps you gain control over your emotions, good and bad.

8

ON-THE-GO MEDITATIONS

KEEP THESE EASY MINDFULNESS TIPS
ON HAND FOR QUICK ACCESS WHENEVER
YOU'RE FEELING OVERWHELMED

→ **TEACHING MEDITATION IN CORPORATE SETTINGS**, I hear many reasons why people don't practice it regularly. The top reason (after "I can't quiet my mind") is "I don't have time." If you have 30 to 60 minutes for meditation daily, that's great, but you can achieve inner peace in five minutes or less. I call these small bursts of mindfulness "micro-meditations," but they're really unclaimed minutes we can put to use to come back to center and hit the reset button. The result: more clarity and calm.

MAKE AN EFFORT TO RECLAIM THESE DOWNTIME MOMENTS IN THE NAME OF MINDFULNESS

1 IN THE SHOWER Breathe slowly, feeling the water hit your body and cleanse your skin. Think of it washing away negativity, stagnation ("stuckness") and anxiety. Add an affirmation, such as "I love my body and enjoy caring for it" or "I wash away anything that does not serve me." Visualize negativity and stress running down through the drain.

2 AT A TRAFFIC LIGHT Sit with your eyes relaxed (not closed) and your hands gently on the wheel or in your lap for the duration of the light. Focus on a mantra—such as "peace" or "stillness"—as you breathe.

3 IN THE DOCTOR'S WAITING ROOM Instead of reading outdated magazines or scrolling through your phone, sit quietly with your eyes closed and your hands in your lap. Breathe deeply and exhale slowly, with the intention of relaxing and quieting the mind. Focus on your body and how it feels, without getting stuck on any one particular sensation. Allow your mind to be open and let your heart expand. Send loving-kindness to others who

are waiting there alongside you or to the office staff, wishing that they would all be free from worry or doubt.

4 RIDING THE ELEVATOR Close your eyes and focus on your breath. Send loving-kindness to your fellow elevator riders and to others working in the building.

5 WHILE WALKING Zen master and monk Thich Nhat Hanh says mindful walking is a profound and pleasurable way to deepen your connection with your body and the Earth. Use the distance from your car to your office for a walking meditation (it's another excuse to park farther away): Soften your gaze and connect with your body as you walk, feeling the contact with the Earth. You might count each step or repeat a mantra such as "peace" with each breath.

6 BEFORE A MEETING Duck in to your meeting a few minutes early to still your mind (especially if you anticipate the occasion being stressful). Gently close your eyes and bring your breath to a slow, steady pace. Breathe into each part of your body, beginning at your toes (with each inhale, imagine breathing relaxation and well-being into that area). Visualize being surrounded by a golden light of peace. Breathe in, allowing peace to flow through your body. Breathe out, exhaling negativity and fear and sending it into the light.

7 IN THE KITCHEN Slow your pace and try to focus on doing one task at a time instead of rushing and multitasking. Become aware of your senses and quietly repeat a mantra such as "nourish," "joy" or "love." Visualize folding the essence of these mantras into the ingredients as you chop, stir and sauté.

8 AS YOU EAT Take a morsel of food, look at it, and smell it. Notice the texture, color and all the different aromas it contains. Put it in your mouth and savor it. Give thanks to all those who contributed to getting this food to your table (farmers, workers and so on). You may find you enjoy it even more!

—*Christi Clemons Hoffman*

Close your eyes and savor the flavor of whatever you're drinking or eating.

WHY LAUGHTER IS THE BEST MEDICINE

WHO NEEDS A PILL WHEN A GOOD GIGGLE CAN BOOST YOUR HEALTH AND HELP YOU FEEL HAPPIER?

→ **YOU DO YOUR BEST** to eat healthy, exercise often and get a good night's sleep whenever possible. But there may be something else missing from your life that can not only boost your health and make you feel better but also increase your mindfulness and enjoy your day.

"Finding ways to laugh every day is key, be it socially or just watching your favorite sitcom in the evening," says Gurinder Bains, Ph.D., professor of allied health studies at Loma Linda University in California. "Laughter really is the best medicine."

If you haven't had a good, loud, snort-inducing chuckle or even a little giggle today, it's okay. But consider how easy it is to enjoy the various benefits of living with a lighter, more positive outlook and genuinely get more laughter in your life.

HEALING POWERS

You may remember the 1998 movie *Patch Adams*, starring Robin Williams as Hunter Campbell, M.D., aka "Patch Adams." In real life, Campbell founded a free hospital in 1971 where he treated patients, incorporating silliness as part of the healing process. Twelve years later, after proving that this concept of a supportive, loving community helped those with both physical and mental illness, Campbell opened Gesundheit Institute, a nonprofit health-care organization in West Virginia.

Since that time, researchers have found that laughter has physiological, psychological, social, spiritual and quality-of-life benefits, according to a review published in the journal *Alternative Therapies in Health and Medicine*. It's been used in everything from oncology to critical care to general patient care and more. Perhaps best of all, there are no negative side effects of using laughter as medicine (unless you count the potential embarrassment of snorting!).

"Laughter can improve one's quality of life mentally, emotionally, socially and physically," Bains says. "Being more social leads to more opportunities to laugh, which leads to less stress, which leads to improving your wellness and eventually an enhancement in your quality of life. It's all connected."

SHARE A GIGGLE

In case you haven't noticed, it's hard to feel bad when you laugh. When that humor is shared with others, our brains release natural opioids, including endorphins. This causes us to feel calmer, more relaxed and better overall while helping to form, reinforce and maintain our social bonds, according to a study published in *The Journal of Neuroscience*.

"The easy, relaxing feeling we get from the opioid release acts as a 'safety signal' telling the brain and body that things are well. This feeling helps us to bond with others—we feel that their company is good for us," explains the study author Lauri Nummenmaa, Ph.D., professor in modeling and medical image processing at the University of Turku in Finland.

Other research from the University of North Carolina has found that we may even be able to assess a relationship based on a couples' laughter. "We found that couples who laughed together more during a conversation tended to report greater overall relationship quality, greater closeness, and greater perceived social support—all key indicators of high quality relationships," says study coauthor and social psychologist Laura Kurtz, Ph.D.

When Kurtz and her coauthor, Sara Algoe, Ph.D., looked at why this may be, they discovered that "shared laughter seems to signal to the laughers that they have something in common—that they're on the same wavelength, so to speak. This increased perception of similarity in turn predicts greater liking for one another and greater desire to get to know one another better," Kurtz explains.

In addition to helping strengthen our relationships, the release of endorphins while

A little levity can go a long way toward helping you stay healthy.

FINDING JOY

Shared laughter is positively associated with strong relationships.

laughing also helps us manage negative emotions. Combine that with a reduction in cortisol and a boost in serotonin and laughter can help reduce depression. In fact, studies suggest that laughter therapy—using humor, playful discovery and appreciation of the absurdity to promote health and wellness—is effective for helping cancer and dialysis patients, the elderly, women with postpartum depression, caregivers and others cope with emotional distress.

YOUNG AT HEART

But mental health isn't the only benefit of laughter. Excess chronic cortisol also alters activity and can damage neurons in the part of the brain called the hippocampus, which is where short-term memory is consolidated. This can lead to impairment in learning and memory, explains Bains.

Luckily, "humor-associated mirthful laughter reduces stress and cortisol—which may mean laughter can aid in improving learning and short-term memory," he adds. However, more research is necessary to determine if laughter can prevent long-term memory loss.

Laughter also is good for our hearts and may have a direct effect on blood vessels. "When we laugh, endorphins interact with receptors on the surface of our blood vessels to release the chemical nitric oxide (NO). NO sends out signals that protect our heart and vascular system by reducing blood pressure and inflammation mediated by LDL ['bad'] cholesterol, and by inhibiting blood clot formation," explains Michael Miller, M.D.,

professor of cardiovascular medicine at the University of Maryland School of Medicine.

HAVE THE LAST LAUGH

You don't need to try open-mic night at the local comedy club to reap all the benefits of getting a good laugh. There are easy ways to give your life some more levity.

● **GET OUT** Since laughter is so social, try to spend more time with others, whether that's with friends, loved ones or colleagues. "We are 30 times more likely to laugh when we are with others rather than when we are alone. Research also shows that we laugh most often in conversations rather than for just jokes or TV shows," Nummenmaa says. "Start having a good chat, and if you choose a topic that's not too serious, laughter is likely to occur."

● **MAKE TIME** "There is some research to suggest that prioritizing the things that make you happy—through how you decide to organize your day-to-day life—can boost your overall positive emotions," Kurtz says. "If you intentionally set aside time for relationships, hobbies or other activities that tend to make you laugh, odds are, you'll experience an uptick in how much laughter you have day in and day out."

● **ENJOY YOUR FAVORITE MEDIA** Don't overlook the giggle power of a good sitcom, funny Instagrammers or a screenshot on your phone that makes you chuckle, says Miller, author of *Heal Your Heart: The Positive Emotions Prescription to Prevent and Reverse Heart Disease*. Then share the fun with friends—after all, why shouldn't they have a good laugh, too?

Spending time with friends and family means you're more likely to get the giggles.

ALL THE WAYS WE LAUGH

THERE ARE DIFFERENT KINDS OF LAUGHTER, AND NOT JUST "HAHA" VERSUS "HEHEHE." SCIENTISTS HAVE IDENTIFIED FIVE CATEGORIES. ONLY SPONTANEOUS AND SELF-INDUCED SEEM TO HAVE HEALTH BENEFITS, AS OUR BRAINS CAN'T TELL THE DIFFERENCE BETWEEN THOSE TWO

→ Spontaneous Laughter
Also called genuine laughter, this is caused by an external stimulus (like a joke or your dog doing something funny) or positive emotions

→ Self-Induced Laughter
This is stimulated laughter—when you laugh at will for no specific reason

→ Stimulated Laughter
Caused by a physical action of external factors, such as being tickled or hitting a "funny bone"

→ Induced Laughter
The result of taking a specific substance, whether that's laughing gas, cannabis, alcohol, caffeine or other drugs

→ Pathological Laughter
This may occur with certain psychiatric disorders and is caused by temporary or permanent neurological diseases that result in injuries to the central nervous system

PET PROJECT

WHY SPENDING TIME WITH YOUR CAT OR DOG CAN TURN ANY FROWN UPSIDE DOWN

→ **A COUPLE OF WEEKS AGO,** I received some bad news. The type of news that makes you question your very being. The type of news, in fact, that makes you want to spend the weekend staring into space, drinking boxed wine and watching *The Real Housewives of Dallas.*

And I did plenty of all those things. But because I was dogsitting for a friend, I also did a lot of other things I probably wouldn't normally have done. Showering and exercising and eating, for example. Sticking to a routine. Those dogs, simply by their furry little existences, somehow made an otherwise unbearable weekend only halfway so.

It's not news that animals can help flip a mood almost instantly. "Research shows that having a pet, or even being around one, can lower heart rate, decrease blood pressure, calm breathing and reduce stress," says psychotherapist Stacy Kaiser, editor at large of *Live Happy* magazine. "This physical reaction helps our emotional well-being. When our bodies are calmer and quieter, our emotional well-being is better and we feel happier overall."

In my job as a dog walker and cat sitter, I see these subtle shifts in my daily outlook just from being around animals. Here's why.

FINDING JOY

Research shows dog owners tend to be healthier than the average person.

1

THEY HELP YOU CHANNEL YOUR INNER ROCK STAR

I've never considered myself a "little dog" person, but that all went out the window when I spent nine nights in a Hello Kitty–themed bed with a Chihuahua named Sunni. She conveyed with her blinky, watery eyes that she loved me so much, it hurt to look at me. I took to carrying her around the house, her tiny legs pointing straight up, her bug eyes fixated on me. "Dogs just want to love you, and that love can be contagious," confirms therapist Aida Vazin, M.A., of Newport Beach, California.

2

THEY GIVE YOUR DAYS STRUCTURE

When I was dog sitting during that infamous weekend, there was something gratifying about needing to get up and feed and walk two cute creatures that were so grateful for my efforts. It made me feel I was doing something productive that day, which had a snowball effect on brightening my mood. "Animals give you a sense of purpose, and when you feel like you're providing for someone outside of yourself, it can't help but make you feel good," says Vazin. Not only that, but it got me walking in the fresh air—another natural mood-booster.

3

THEY EXPAND YOUR SOCIAL CIRCLE

My neighbor Leslie, a 60-something woman in my condo community, walks her dog, Sonny, several times a day. In an era when people barely greet their neighbors, we've gotten to know each other in a way that we likely wouldn't have otherwise. She's become a central part of my community, and I have her dog to thank for bringing her into my life. This, says Vazin, is one of the unexpected bonuses of pets. "Animals can be a conversation piece and can bring people together," she says.

4

THEY CHANGE YOUR PERSPECTIVE

It never fails: I set out on my walk with "the usual suspects" occupying my mind: bills, deadlines, that last conversation I had with a friend. But within 10 minutes, I have a purring tabby with huge green eyes named Kitty Pie on my shoulders as we tour the windows. A half hour later, I'm playing ball with a goofy golden retriever named Layla. Soon I'm watching Rudy the chiweenie strut his stuff down the street. One doesn't need research to explain how a day like this can't help but cheer up the mood.

5

THEY HELP YOU CLEAR YOUR MIND

You know that whole "great idea that came to me in the shower" phenomenon? Same deal when caring for pets: I find my best ideas pop into my mind when I'm playing ball with a dog or even cleaning out a litter box. They also breathe fresh life into my surroundings; while they're sniffing, they're allowing me to take stock of the scenery instead of charging full steam ahead. "Animals allow us to get out of our heads when we're consumed by our little thought bubbles," Vazin says.

While I've been "between animals" for a number of years now (R.I.P. 2014 to my brown tabby Lily, R.I.P. 2015 to my yellow Lab Luey), I've found that simply being around animals makes me happier. I like to think of my clients as my furry Zen masters. I mean, it's hard not to smile when thinking about Pepper the cattle dog chasing me around the dining room table, Merlin the poodle's prancy walk, Voici the brown tabby perfecting his red-dot-hunting skills or Vern the dachshund's hilarious tiny steps. And don't even get me started again on Sunni's Chihuahua eyes. Can you blame me, though? After all, I'm only human.

—*Megan McMorris*

Dog person? Cat person? No matter which, an animal can give you a sense of purpose.

One theory is that dogs lick us to show love—and the feeling is usually mutual.

FIND YOUR PERFECT MATCH

READY TO ADD A FURRY FRIEND TO YOUR HOUSEHOLD?
WE ASKED HOLISTIC VET LAURIE COGER, D.V.M.,
IN ALBANY, NEW YORK, FOR SOME HINTS ON MAKING SURE
YOU'VE FOUND YOUR BEST MATE

1

Discover Your True Pet Personality

It's easy to pinpoint what type of animal you've always been interested in, but try expanding your mindset. "Clients often come in with what appears to be a disconnect between the owner and the dog, and it's because they are actually cat people at heart, and they just don't realize it, but the dog can tell!" Coger says. Or if you always think that you're a large dog person, consider acquainting yourself with a smaller pooch.

2

Do Some Research

It makes sense to go online to look for that precious pooch or cuddly cat. Websites like Petfinder (petfinder.com), the ASPCA (aspca.org) and Best Friends (bestfriends.org) will let you click and search for potential local adoptees.

3

Size Up Your Social Skills

"One of the biggest things people overlook when considering a pet is how they prefer to socialize," says Coger. If you're the type who wants to bring your dog to hang out, try a friendly retriever or Lab. Enjoy entertaining at home? Make sure your cat is equally outgoing so you're not creating some undue stress.

4

Consider Your Lifestyle

You've always felt drawn to that adorable border collie, but be honest with yourself: Do you really have the time and energy it would take to stimulate a working breed? Make sure your lifestyle—including time, budget and living and working situation—and your new pet's needs will match up before getting in over your head.

INDEX

A

Action patterns/plans, 124–127
Advice, well-meaning, 71
Age groups, contentment and, 40–47
Animals. See also Pets
  therapy dogs, 139
Austria, 29

B

Baby, happiness conundrum and, 76
Bad mood, tips to dispel, 137–141
Bathing, 138
Beaches, 133
Being happy
  health benefits of, 16–23
  individual variations in, 8–13
  perceived pressure for, 11, 13, 34
Biking to work, 113
Blessings, counting your, 14, 54
Brain
  boost for, 18
  challenges for, 141
  exercise and, 141
  hugging and, 152
Breathing, mindful, 63, 70, 103, 113, 126, 168–169
  meditation and, 161, 162, 164

C

Canada, 29
Career/Job
  commuting time and, 113
  finding meaning in, 104–109
  happiness conundrum and, 80–81
  negative colleagues and, 71–72
  pride in week's work, 103
  satisfaction indicators, 111
  stress of, 42, 70
Change, embracing, 64–65
Charitable donations, 134
Cheerful children, 82–89
Cheerfulness, tips to achieve, 137–141
Children
  as happiness conundrum/plan, 76
  joyful, how to raise, 82–89
Chocolate, dark, 134
Clarity of thought
  decluttering and, 116
  pets and, 182
Common cold
  positive feelings and, 18
  regular hugging and, 153, 155
Commuting time, 113
Complaining, 72, 139
Contentment, maximizing, 40–47
Cortisol levels, 20, 161, 175
"Cuddle" hormone, 152
"Cuddle Party," 157

D

Daily routine, pets and, 181
Dark chocolate, 134
Decluttering (Marie Kondo method), 114–121
Decorating strategies, for mindful living space, 120–121
Denmark, 28
Depression, 21
  exercise and, 149
  in friend, coping with, 70
  hugs alleviating, 152
  laughter reducing, 175
  in parents, 85
  pressure to be happy and, 11, 13, 34
  signs of, 35
Displeasure/Distress,
  happiness conundrum and, 74–81
Downtime moments, 168
Drinking water, 136
Driving to work, 113

E

"E.A.S.Y." meditation method, 161–162
Economic factors, happiness levels and, 26
Emotions, positive:negative ratio, 36. See also Negative emotions/experiences; Positive feelings
Empathy, 69, 72
Employment. See Career/Job
Endocannabinoids, 149
Endorphins, 149
  laughter and, 175
  positive feelings and, 18, 20
Essential oils, 134
Exercise, 135

mental health benefits,
142–149
mindfulness and, 145–146
as mood booster, 15
resilience and, 62
Expectations
job/career, 42
setting for self, 43
societal and cultural, 45

F

Facebook, 34, 42
Fatherhood, happiness
conundrum and, 76–80
Fears, facing your, 63
Feeling blue, 20, 70
clinical depression vs., 21, 35
Fight-or-flight response, 20,
161
Finances, conflict and, 68, 70
Finland, 29
Flowers, 141
Food, protein-rich, 135
Friend, depression in, 70
Fulfillment, finding, 98–127

G

Games, 141
Gesundheit Institute, 172
Global joy, 24–31
Good deeds, 136
Gratefulness, 54, 132
Gray area, emotional, 36

H

Happiness. See Being happy;
World Happiness Report
Happiness conundrum, 74–81

Healing
laughter and, 172
physical touch and, 152–153
Health benefits, 16–23
exercise and, 146
laughter and, 175
pets and, 179
Healthy coping methods, 138
Heart health
laughter and, 175
positive feelings and, 18
Heart rate, 18, 145
Hippocampus, 149, 175
Hobby(ies)
developing new, 45
as mood-booster, 13, 15, 39,
175
Home
decluttering/organizing,
114–121
location importance, 90–94
relocation strategies, 95–97
Hugging, 150–157
Humor. See Laughter
Hydrating, 136

I

Iceland, 28
Immune system, mood
and, 18, 22
Induced laughter, 177
Instagram, 34, 175
Intentionality
commuting time and, 113
exercise and, 146
kindness and, 53
laughter and, 175
upcoming workweek and, 102

J

Job. See Career/Job
Journal, keeping a, 132
Joy
acknowledging, 140
finding in everyday life,
98–127
measuring globally,
24–31
Joyful children, 82–89

K

Kindness, 50–57
acts of, 52, 56–57
cultivating, 54
meaning of, 53
teaching to children, 84
Knitting, 15

L

Laughter
benefits of, 170–175
types of, 177
ways to increase, 175
Laughter therapy, 175
Learning, laughter and, 175
Life balance, restoring, 116
Life phases, 41–47
Life satisfaction, 134
happiest countries, 28–30
least happy countries, 31
Literature, reading, 132
Living space, mindful,
120–121
Loneliness, 46
Longevity, 22, 55
Loving-kindness meditation
method, 164

INDEX

M

Marriage, happiness conundrum and, 76

Media
laughter and, 175
negative news, 140

Meditation
methods, 161–165
mindfulness and, 161
as mood-booster, 15
on-the-go, 166–169

Memory, laughter and, 175

Mental health benefits
exercise and, 142–148
laughter and, 172–175

Micro meditations, 166

Mindful breathing meditation method, 162

Mindfulness, 158–165
defined, 161
exercise and, 145–146
living space and, 120–121
meditation methods, 161–165
places to practice, 168–169
resilience and, 63

Mistakes, making, 84

"Monday blahs," 100–103

Money, conflict and, 68, 70

Mood
immune system and, 22
improvement tips, 131–141
music and, 137
pets and, 179
positive feelings and, 22
strategies for boosting, 14–15

Motherhood, happiness conundrum and, 76–80

Music, mood and, 137

N

National Hugging Day, 152

Negative emotions/experiences, 33–39
caught in traffic, 113
navigational strategies, 33–39
sharing with others, 10–11

Negative news, tuning out, 140

Negativity
coping with, 68–73
purpose of, 34, 36

Netherlands, 29

New Zealand, 29

Nitric oxide (NO), laughter and, 175

Norway, 28

O

Ocean views, 133

Older people, contentment and, 46–47

On-the-go meditations, 166–169

Opportunity, 36

Optimism, 84

Organizing (Marie Kondo method), 114–121

Outdoors, exercise in, 145

Oxytocin, 152

P

Pain, 10–11, 22

Parenting happiness gap, 77

Parents
depression in, 85
negative comments from, 70–71, 72

Patch Adams (movie), 172

Pathological laughter, 177

Perfectionism, 84

Pets
benefits of, 178–183
choosing, tips on, 184–185

Physical activity. See Exercise; individually named activities

Physical touch, 150–157

Place, importance of, 90–93

Pleasures, simple, 128–185

Positive feelings
body's responses to, 118
health benefits of, 16–23

Positive:negative emotion ratio, 36

Positivity, 18, 85
maintaining, 66–73
start of workweek, 102–103

Practicing presence meditation method, 162–164

Pressure
to be happy, 11, 13, 34
job/career expectations and, 42
parenting expectations and, 77–78

Procrastination, 124–127

Protein-rich foods, 135

PTSD (post-traumatic stress disorder), 139

Public transport, 113

Purpose, sense of, 46–47
  finding, 64
  volunteering and, 55
  at work, 102

R

Reading, 102, 132
Recipes, new, 141
Relationships
  cultivating, 42
  maintaining, 47
  money conflicts in, 68, 70
Relocation strategies, 95–97
Resilience, importance of,
  58–65
Retirement, 46

S

Sadness. See Depression;
  Feeling blue
Satisfaction. See also Life
  satisfaction
  career/job, 111
  task completion, 125
Scents, 134
Science of happiness, 8–13
Self-care, 72
Self-criticism, 36, 146
Self-determination, 10
Self-induced laughter, 177
Sentimental items, 119
Serotonin
  laughter and, 161, 175
  positive feelings and, 18
Shared laughter, 173–175
Silliness, 172
Sleep, 22
Smiles, producing, 131–141

Social factors, happiness
  levels and, 26
Social interaction
  happiness research and,
  9–13
  laughter and, 175, 176
  as mood booster, 15
  pets and, 182
Social media, 34, 42,
  125, 175
Social network, 62
Spontaneous laughter, 177
Stimulated laughter, 177
Stress relief
  decluttering as, 114–121
  exercise and, 143–148
  laughter and, 175
  resilience and, 60
  volunteering and, 54
Stress response, 20
Sweden, 29
Switzerland, 28

T

Tactile stimulation, 152
"Talk Test," 145
Thank-you notes, 54
Therapy dogs, 139
Time commitment, 54
To-do lists, 124, 125
Touch, importance of,
  150–157
Tough situations/times
  resilience and, 58–65
  staying positive in,
  66–73
Traffic, caught in, 113
T.R.A.P. technique, 126

U

United States
  happiest cities, 92
  happiness ranking, 26–27

V

Vacation planning, 132
Volunteering, 46, 52

W

Waking routine, 139
Walking, 113, 135
Water, drinking, 136
Weight sensitivity, 72–73
Well-being, 10, 18
  in old age, 46
  pets and, 179
  volunteering and, 46
Willpower, 85
Work. See Career/Job
Workplace, 104–108
Workspace, 103
Workweek, starting the,
  100–103
World Happiness Report, 26,
  29
  happiest countries, 27,
  28–30
  happiness indicators,
  26–27
  job satisfaction indicators,
  111
  least happy countries, 26,
  29, 31
Writing, 132

Y

Yoga, 63, 103, 145

CREDITS

COVER Mego Studio/Shutterstock 4-5 SolStock/Getty Images 6-7 JGI/Jamie Grill/Getty Images 8-9 Alexander Rieber/EyeEm/Getty Images 11 SDI Productions/Getty Images 12-13 SDI Productions/Getty Images 16-17 (Clockwise from top left) wundervisuals/Getty Images; Maskot/Getty Images; wundervisuals/Getty Images; Peathegee Inc/Getty Images 18-19 Hero Images/Getty Images 21 Martin Dimitrov/Getty Images 22-23 Uwe Krejci/Getty Images 24-25 Robin Skjoldborg/Getty Images 27 Thanasis Zovoilis/Getty Images 28 (From top) kupicoo/Getty Images; Maximilian Stock Ltd./Getty Images 29 Maskot/Getty Images 30 (Clockwise from top left) bodrumsurf/Getty Images; mehmetbuma/Getty Images; bodrumsurf/Getty Images; Poligrafistka/Getty Images; -ELIKA-/Getty Images; Image Source/Getty Images; Poligrafistka/Getty Images; Sveta_Aho/Getty Images; MicroStockHub/Getty Images; MicroStockHub/Getty Images; bodrumsurf/Getty Images 31 (Clockwise from top left) bodrumsurf/Getty Images; liangpv/Getty Images; Kypros/Getty Images; Poligrafistka/Getty Images (3); kosmozoo/Getty Images (2); Kypros/Getty Images; kosmozoo/Getty Images; bodrumsurf/Getty Images 32 Aknur Akhmetova/EyeEm/Getty Images 34-35 praetorianphoto/Getty Images 37 JGI/Jamie Grill/Getty Images 38-39 Tetra Images/Getty Images 40 Paul Bradbury/Getty Images 42 portishead1/Getty Images 43 Kelvin Murray/Getty Images 44 Sally Anscombe/Getty Images 46 Jose Luis Pelaez Inc/Getty Images 47 Abel Mitja Varela/Morsa Images/Getty Images 48-49 Christopher Hopefitch/Getty Images 50 Jordan Siemens/Getty Images 53 Compassionate Eye Foundation/Andrew Olney/Getty Images 55 Hill Street Studios/Eric Raptosh/Getty Images 56-57 Hero Images/Getty Images 58-59 Digital Vision./Getty Images 60-61 Thomas Barwick/Getty Images 64-65 Darryl Leniuk/Getty Images 66-67 Chris Bailey/Getty Images 69 Tetra Images/Getty Images 73 wakila/Getty Images 74 Tabor Gus/Corbis/VCG 76-77 AleksanderNakic/iStockphoto 79 Annie Otzen/Getty Images 81 FatCamera/Getty Images 82-83 Lumi Images/Dario Secen/Getty Images 85 Hero Images/Getty Images 86-87 PeopleImages/Yuri_Arcurs/Getty Images 90-91 Thomas Barwick/Getty Images 93 Portra/Getty Images 94 Thomas Barwick/Getty Images 96-97 Imgorthand/Getty Images 98-99 Westend61/Getty Images 100-101 PeopleImages/Getty Images 104-105 Geber86/Getty Images 107 PeopleImages/Getty Images 109 Kelvin Murray/Getty Images 110-111 Corey Jenkins/Getty Images 112 RyanJLane/Getty Images 114-115 Westend61/Getty Images 117 Jessica Peterson/Getty Images 118-119 Fancy/Veer/Corbis/Getty Images 122-123 Image Source/Getty Images 124 Andrew Kolb/Getty Images 127 Gary John Norman/Getty Images 128-129 WANDER WOMEN COLLECTIVE/Getty Images 130-131 shapecharge/Getty Images 132 Tetra Images/Jessica Peterson/Getty Images 133 Jessie Casson/Getty Images 134 (From top) Creative Crop/Getty Images; Walker and Walker/Getty Images 135 Hero Images/Getty Images 136 (From left) grandriver/Robert Ingelhart/Getty Images; christianpound/Getty Images 137 Westend61/Getty Images 138 Hero Images/Getty Images 139 Flashpop/Getty Images 140 Hero Images/Getty Images 141 jonathansloane/Getty Images 142-143 People Images/Getty Images 144 Mint Images RF/Getty Images 146-147 milan2099/Getty Images 150 Flashpop/Brand New Images Ltd/Getty Images 153 PeopleImages/Getty Images 154-155 filadendron/Getty Images 157 Caiaimage/Trevor Adeline/Getty Images 158-159 Joe Morahan/Getty Images 160 Ingo Roesler/Getty Images 163 Mikolette/Getty Images 165 swissmediavision/Getty Images 166-167 d3sign/Getty Images 169 BraunS/Getty Images 170-171 SolStock/Getty Images 173 Chris Cross/ Getty Images 174 SolStock/Getty Images 176-177 Hero Images/Getty Images 178-179 (Center) Life On White/Eric Isselee/Getty Images (Clockwise from top left) Jamie Grill/Getty Images Dorling Kindersley/Getty Images; JW LTD/Getty Images; Steve Shott/Getty Images; Uwe Krejci/Getty Images; Steve Shott/Getty Images; Catherine Ledner/Getty Images; ULTRA.F/Getty Images 180-183 Martin Barraud/Getty Images (2) 184 Hero Images/Getty Images

SPECIAL THANKS TO CONTRIBUTING WRITERS:
Christi Clemons Hoffman, Locke Hughes, Diana Kelly Levey, Megan McMorris,
Brittany Risher, Katherine Schreiber and Celia Shatzman

CENTENNIAL BOOKS

An Imprint of
Centennial Media, LLC
40 Worth St., 10th Floor
New York, NY 10013, U.S.A.

CENTENNIAL BOOKS is a trademark of Centennial Media, LLC

ISBN 978-1-951274-11-5

Distributed by
Simon & Schuster, Inc.
1230 Avenue of the Americas
New York, NY 10020, U.S.A.

For information about custom editions, special sales, and premium and corporate purchases,
please contact Centennial Media at contact@centennialmedia.com.

Manufactured in China

Publishers & Co-Founders Ben Harris, Sebastian Raatz
Editorial Director Annabel Vered
Creative Director Jessica Power
Executive Editor Janet Giovanelli
Design Director Ben Margherita
Senior Art Director Laurene Chavez
Art Directors Natali Suasnavas, Joseph Ulatowski
Production Manager Paul Rodina
Production Assistant Alyssa Swiderski
Editorial Assistant Tiana Schippa